W9-CER-452

DOCTOR WHO

THE OFFICIAL DOCTIONARY

BBC Children's Books
Published by the Penguin Group
Penguin Books Ltd, 80 Strand, London, WC2R 0RL, England
Penguin Group (USA) Inc., 375 Hudson Street, New York 10014, USA
Penguin Books (Australia) Ltd, 250 Camberwell Road, Camberwell,
Victoria 3124, Australia
(A division of Pearson Australia Group PTY Ltd)
Penguin Group (NZ), 67 Apollo Drive, Rosedale, Auckland
0632, New Zealand (a division of Pearson New Zealand Ltd)
Canada, India, South Africa
Published by BBC Children's Books, 2012

Written by Justin Richards
Edited by Jason Loborik
Designed by Jason McEvoy

001 - 10 9 8 7 6 5 4 3 2 1

BBC, DOCTOR WHO (word marks, logos and devices), TARDIS, DALEKS, CYBERMAN and K-9 (word marks and devices)
are trade marks of the British Broadcasting Corporation and are used under licence.
ISBN: 9781405908962
Printed in China

Istock: © Christian Miller, Sébastien Decoret p.8; pederk p.9; Martin Adams p.10; Heidi Kristensen, parameter p.11; Sébastien Decoret, parameter p.12; Lars Lentz p.13; Baris Simsek p.14-15; Robert Skold, loops7, Christian Miller p.16; parameter p.17; Tran The Vuong p.19; cosmin4000 p.36; Andrey Prokhorov p.49; loops7 p.147; serts p.161; Georgina Palmer p.164; Martin McCarthy p.168; Bob Ingelhart p.169
Science Photo Library p.31
Shutterstock.com: © Neftali p.166

THE OFFICIAL DOCTIONARY

Doctionary *(essential book)* the Doctor's dictionary of definitions for time travellers

Contents

THE DOCTIONARY

Introduction

Do you ever have moments when you wonder what someone else is talking about? I do. But then I have moments when I wonder what I'm talking about. So do other people, it seems. 'What is he talking about?' they wonder as I rattle on about… Well, about whatever it is I'm rattling on about.

So I thought, wouldn't it be great if I had a list of lots of the things I say and explanations of what I mean? What I usually mean. Sometimes.

Then everyone would know what I'm on about, and I'd be able to check that it all makes sense. Sort of. A bit. Perhaps.

Anyway, whether it's useful or not, here it is. I hope it helps. If not, then – er – sorry. But I've got to dash. There's a bit of bother in the Gatikarian Galaxy that needs sorting out. Something to do with a Sontaran, a bottle of fizzy drink, a bath plug and a trombone.

Talk to you soon. Or 'Vastan der Moibles' as they say in Eutacaria Fourteen. On Wednesdays. Whatever it means.

The Doctor

Space and Astronomy and Stuff

If you're going to be a space traveller, and why not, then you need to know this stuff. If nothing else, so you can work out where you are, or what you were just hit by.

Asteroid

It's like this big rock thing floating in space. Well, not that big – I mean, not planet-sized big. More sort of small-big really. And actually, 'floating' isn't right because you sort of do that in water or liquid and space is, well, space. Space is pretty much full of floaty rock things, except it's called space because it's so empty.

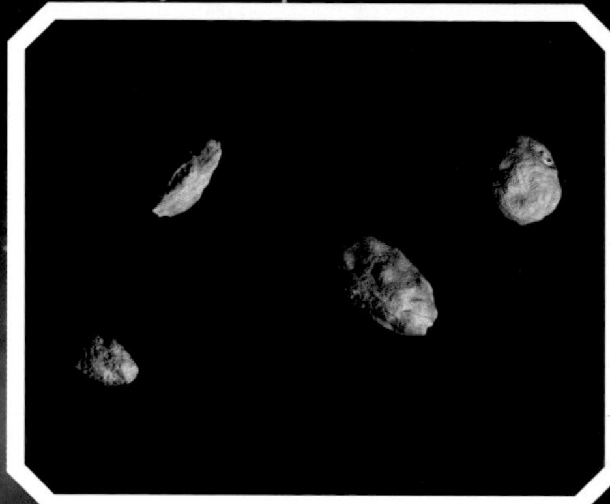

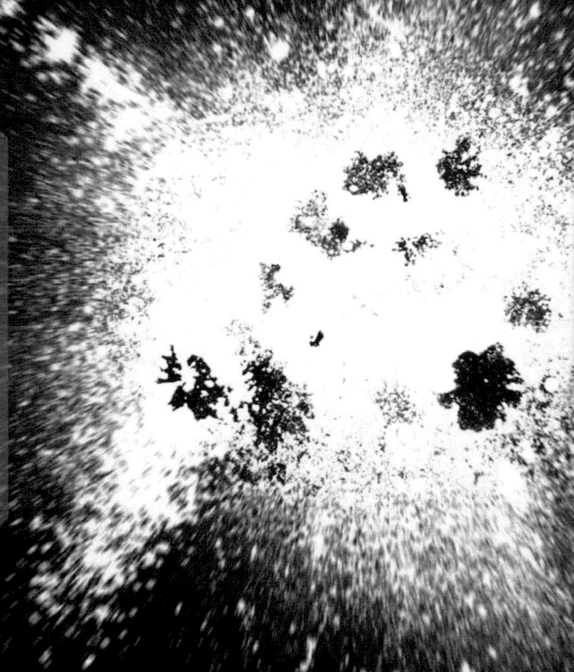

Big Bang, the

I was there. No, really. Right at the start – because that's what the Big Bang was. It's when the universe just started from nothing. Except when it started again from an exploding TARDIS but that was different. Start of the universe, then – bang, and there it was. Small at first, but expanding and getting bigger and bigger.

Black Hole

It's not a hole and not black. But otherwise 'black hole' sums it up pretty well really. It's what you get when an old star collapses in on itself and the gravity is just so strong that everything gets crushed up really tiny – shunk! – like that. The gravity is so strong that everything round it gets pulled in and crunched-up and nothing can get out. Not even light. Which is why it's black. It's not really black, it's just there's no light. So dark maybe. Yeah, that's it – a 'Dark Crunch'.

Dwarf Star

Right, well, before it becomes a black hole the star gets really heavy because of the crunch-up thing. Compressed matter. You can make Dwarf Star Alloy out of the material and that's just really super strong and nothing can get through it. Which is useful.

Jupiter

As planets go, Jupiter is a big one. Really – huge. Biggest in the Solar System. Your human solar system that is, of course. Big chap – what's called a gas giant. That's because, well, it's made of gas – mostly hydrogen with some helium thrown in. And it's big. What else do you need to know? Fifth planet out from the sun. Lot of moons. And a big Red Spot which is actually a storm that's been raging for centuries and is bigger than the Earth. Got that? A storm that is Bigger – Than – The – Earth.

Mars

Not as big as Jupiter. As planets go, pretty average really – fourth from the sun. About half the size of Earth. Just don't drink the water – if you find any. Really, avoid. Mars used to be home to the Martians, which sort of makes sense. I nicknamed them Ice Warriors because they like the cold. Big armoured lizard things with a keen sense of honour and a love of war. Which is appropriate, because Mars is named after the Roman god of war. So there you go.

Mercury

Tiny planet. And hot. Closest to the sun, so burny-wurny and then some. Probably why I've never been there. But one day I will, I'm sure. It's on my list. You got a list? Everyone should have a list.

Meteor

Big rock in space. Yes, OK, sort of like an asteroid. But smaller. Well, actually they're called 'meteoroids' by Science People these days (in your time, I mean). They say now that a 'meteor' is the trail a meteoroid leaves through the atmosphere as it burns up. No, not actually in space at all really. But if you say meteor most people know what you mean. Which is meteoroid.

Meteoroid

Hang on, we just did this one. Read 'Meteor' again if you still haven't got it.

Moons in general

Bits of rock in space that go round other bigger bits of rock in space. Or balls of gas – moons can go round those, too. So sort of like asteroids or meteoroids but in orbit round a planet. Or another moon, I suppose. You could have a moon's moons. At least I think so.

Moon, the

By 'the' Moon we – or rather you humans – mean the moon that orbits planet Earth. Or one of them, because there are lots of tiddly ones as well as that great big one that you see up in the sky and where Neil Armstrong made his one small step. It's got a lot to answer for, though. Sent the ancient reptile people of Earth scurrying for cover when it turned up and got caught in Earth's orbit. And then there are werewolves.

Neptune

Another planet in your solar system. Eighth from the sun. So, furthest out, if you don't count Pluto (and people don't these days, which is a pity). It looks very blue, which is nice because it's named after the god of the sea. Though it's blue because of methane not water, but you can't have everything, can you?

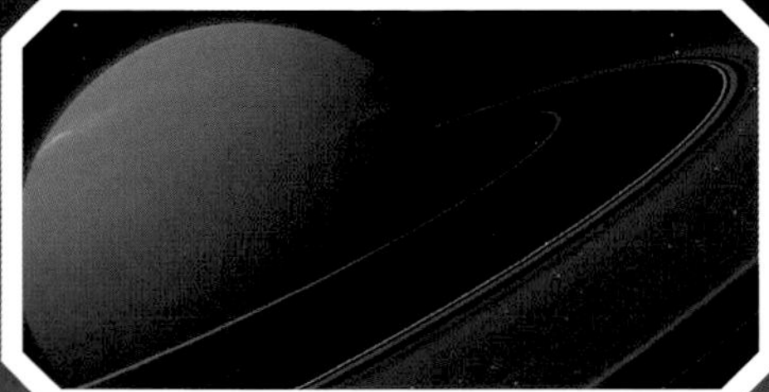

Planet

What we've been talking about – big rock or gas things in space that go round a sun or star like moons go round planets. You know what – for stuff like this, alphabetical order is just rubbish.

Planetoid

Well, it's a little tiny planet really, isn't it? I mean, really tiny – smaller than Pluto (coming up next – no more spoilers). Probably too small to bother with really. I mean, when you're discovering over 3,000 of these a month just in your own solar system, which you are, you have ask yourself: Why bother?

Pluto

Yes! Been there, though not yet. It was a lovely sunny place. Though not yet. Far far out from the sun, so dark and cold at the moment. And demoted – used to be a planet but now the people who decide what planets are (and who does that? I mean, really?) have decided that Pluto is a 'dwarf planet'. Well, I'm sorry to be picky here but a dwarf planet is just a small planet isn't it? So why not call it a planet and make sure people know it's small? Job done.

Saturn

Another planet – and no doubt about this one because it's a biggie. Second largest (after Jupiter, remember?) and sixth out from the sun. Best known for its impressive rings. Also has moons. I blew one of them up once (well, not yet I didn't). But it was the only way, trust me – bit of trouble with a giant sentient virus swarm.

Sol 3

That's your sun in Time Lord Speak. No, really – Sol 3 in Mutter's Spiral. There you go. You've got an address and everything now for the human race. The Earth, The Solar System, Sol 3, Mutter's Spiral, Western Spiral Arm, Milky Way, The Universe. Not sure of the postcode, and put extra stamps on just to be sure.

Solar System

A set of planets that go round a sun. So in that delightfully human-centric way you humans have, 'the' Solar System is the set of planets that includes Earth going round your sun.

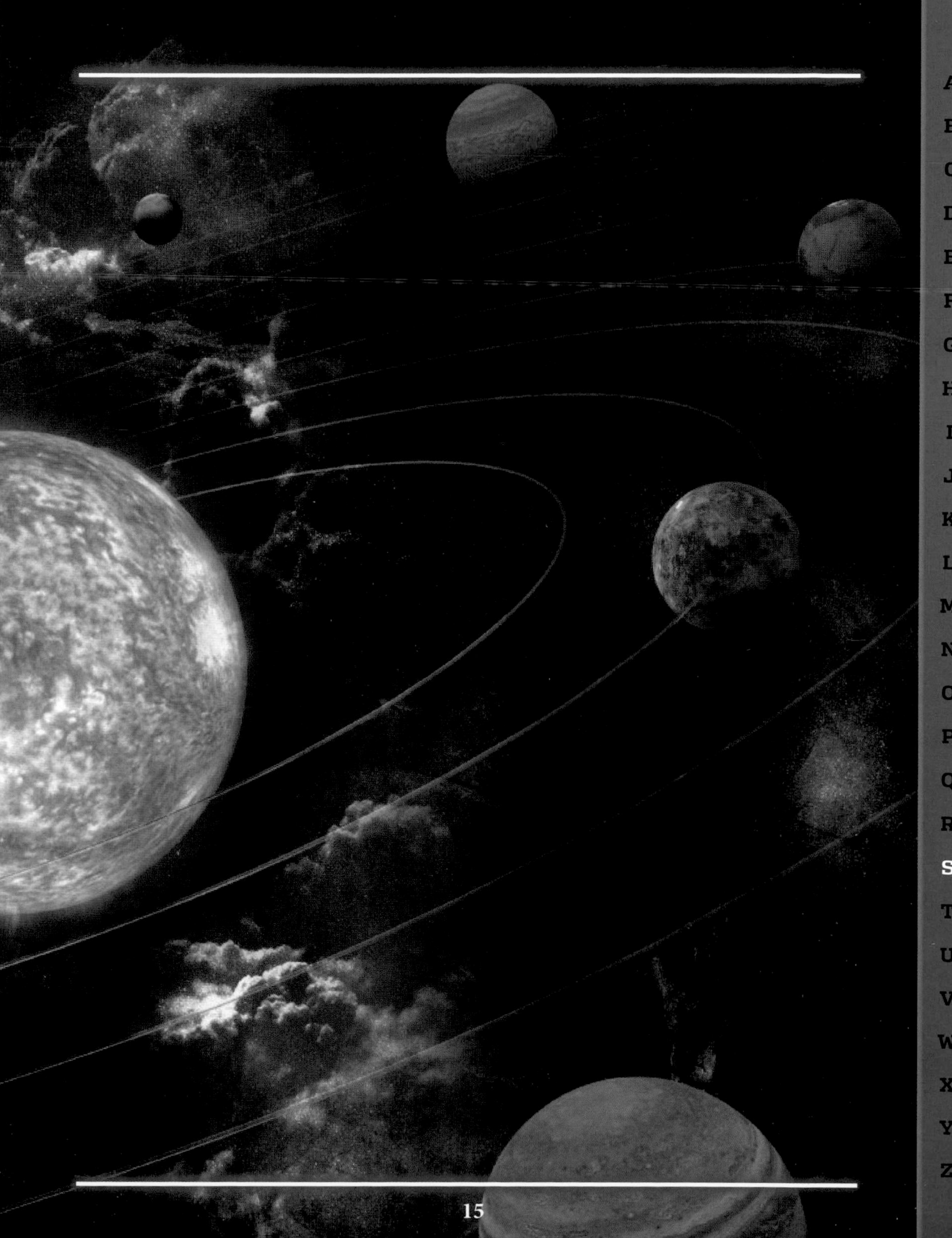

A B C D E F G H I J K L M N O P Q R S T U V W X Y Z

Star

Another human-centric thingy. You have your own sun, but anyone else's sun is called a star. A bit spacist if you ask me, but that's how it goes. Oh, and then you like to categorise your stars into different sorts – dwarfs and whitepoints and variables, and different classes with really boring names that only a human could think up like 'O Class' or 'B Class' and other random letters.

Uranus

Not funny at all, but it really is pronounced like that no matter what the Americans might think. They're just embarrassed and have no sense of humour. How can they have a sense of something they can't even spell? Sorry, where was I? Oh yes – another planet. Yawn. Uranus was the Greek god of the sky, which I guess makes sense. Slow and dim – so a bit like an Ogron. Sorry, joke. Moving on…

Universe

Everything. All of it – the whole lot. Everywhere. So all the stars in the sky and in everyone else's sky together with all their planets and stuff. Even non-stuff, which we call space, is part of the everything that we call the universe. So there's nothing that isn't in the universe. Nothing at all. Except other universes. Um, OK, let's skip that for now – the universe is everything, right. Except for the other stuff.

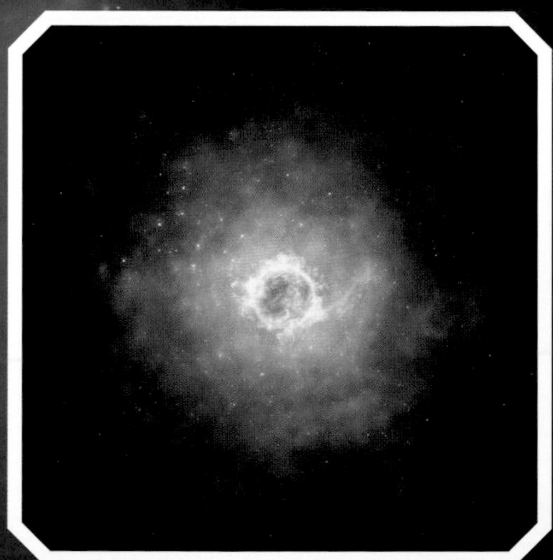

Venus

Oh boring! How many more of these planet things are there? (I've just skipped ahead, and this is the last one – so don't worry.) Anyway, briefly – second planet out from the sun, and about the same size as Earth, because I know how you humans like to compare everything to your own planet. Can't think why.

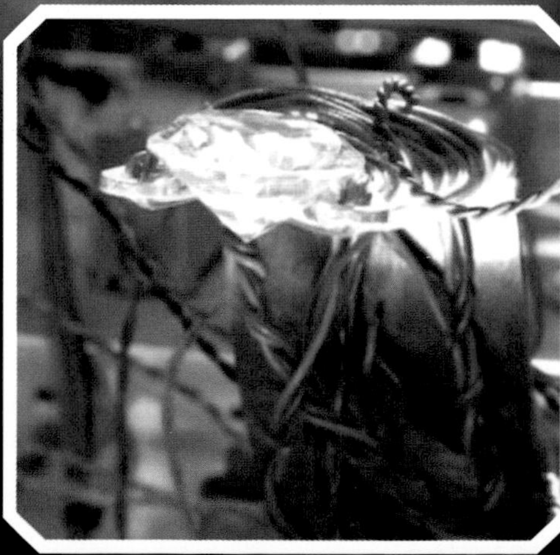

Whitepoint Star

You don't find many of these – very rare. Look like diamonds. Big, expensive, beautiful diamonds. President Rassilon had one, which he used to create a link from time-locked Gallifrey to Earth. Very special things, Whitepoint Stars. All sorts of capabilities. So best avoided really.

Time and Relative Dimensions in Space

If you're going to travel through space and time, then there's loads more stuff you need to know. 'Stuff' is a technical term. It means like things. OK, got that? Things. There's lots more stuff/things you'll need to know, but this should get you started.

Academy, the

School for Time Lords. On Gallifrey in the Old Days we all had to go to an Academy. I was at Prydon Academy, so that made me a Prydonian. So was the Master, but we won't dwell on that. Prydon produced more Time Lord Presidents than any other Academy, including me. But that was a mistake, in oh so many ways…

Blinovitch Limitation Effect, the

When there's timey-wimey trouble, likely as not it's because of the Blinovitch Limitation Effect. That's what stops you going back and changing the past so things work out all right in the present. Because if you could do that, then everything would just be too confusing for words. I can do it, obviously – sometimes. Well, now and then. Mostly 'then' to be honest.

Blue Stabilisers

Not to be confused with Red Stabilisers – that could be very dangerous. And embarrassing. If there's one thing worse than dangerous, then it's embarrassing. Believe me.

Chameleon Circuit

You know how the TARDIS changes its shape every time it lands so as to blend in with the surroundings? So if it lands in a forest it will look like a tree, and if it ever landed in a quarry (not likely) it might look like a big rock or something. No? Well, that's because the Chameleon Circuit, which makes it blend in like that, is broken. Has been for ages. Ever since the TARDIS landed in London in the 1960s and changed to look like a Police Telephone Box. I could fix it, I tried once. But actually I quite like her looking like a Police Telephone Box. Don't lose her nearly as often now.

Cloister Bell

The Cloister Bell is another TARDIS thing. It's a bell, well a sort of 'chime' really, that sounds when the TARDIS is in real danger. And I mean really in real danger. Not sure why it's called the Cloister Bell, though. You can hear it in the TARDIS Cloisters, but then again you can hear it all over the TARDIS. Must be a reason though.

Dark Times of Gallifrey

Long ago, when even Rassilon was young, and before all that time travel malarkey – that's what we call the Dark Times. Billions of years ago. They weren't really dark, of course. Any more than on Earth the Dark Ages were actually dark. Well, except at night. Obviously.

Dimensionally Transcendental

You know how the TARDIS is bigger on the inside than it is on the outside? Course you do, people keep going on about it. Well, that's because it's dimensionally transcendental. Which means it's bigger inside than out – a key Time Lord technology. Basically it's because the TARDIS is a three-dimensional projection of a four-dimensional object into a three -dimensional universe. See – easy.

Fast Return Switch

On no account press this switch in the TARDIS. It's supposed to whiz you back to where you were. Or something. Not sure, actually – and anyway it's broken. The spring sticks, so it ends up whizzing you back and back and back, and then even further back. So, you know – don't. I've labelled it in felt-tip pen to remind me never to touch it.

Harmonic Filter

Another TARDIS thingy. Quite clever though – if you feed gravity patterns through it they come out as music. How cool is that? I've got no idea what it's really for though.

Idris

I don't really know who Idris was, I'm afraid. She was kept alive by House until it filled her with the soul of the TARDIS. My TARDIS. My poor TARDIS. But Idris – or TARDIS – helped me get things sorted out and put her back where she's supposed to be.

Omega

You could call Omega the first ever Time Lord. He was the stellar engineer who provided the power the Time Lords needed to make time travel work. To do this he exploded a star, but he was lost in the resulting super nova. We all thought he was dead, but he ended up inside the black hole that resulted from the super nova collapsing. And he wasn't very happy that his own people had given up on him. Went a bit bonkers, actually. So I had to sort him out. Twice.

Rassilon

Ah, now Rassilon really was the first Time Lord – or the first great Time Lord. Pretty much wrote the laws of time, founded Time Lord society, became the first President and gave his name to all sorts of things. Then the Great Time War happened, and nothing has ever been the same since.

Regeneration

When a Time Lord's body wears out or is badly damaged, Regeneration is the process we use to get a new one. All the cells in the body get shifted round – which, I have to tell you is not a very pleasant experience – and the result is that the Time Lord ends up looking completely different. But alive, which is a definite bonus. Of course, if a Time Lord is actually properly killed dead, then that's it. Dead. And you only get so many regenerations, so don't waste them!

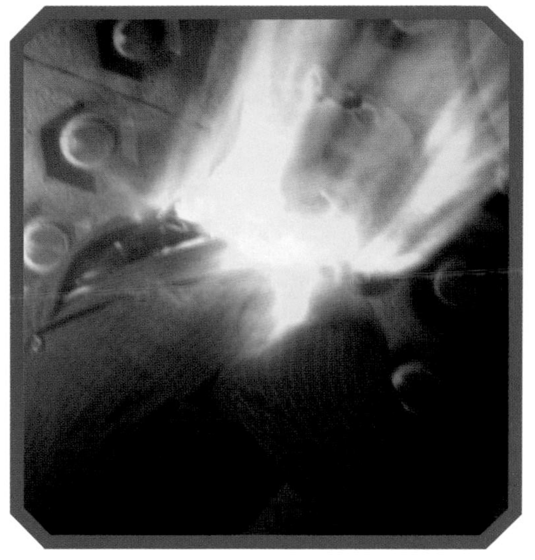

Roundel

Roundels are those circular indentations in the TARDIS walls. Some of them are actually access panels for circuitry and control systems and stuff. Don't know who called them roundels, or why, but that's what they're called. Because they're round, I suppose.

TARDIS

Time And Relative Dimension In Space – TARDIS. There you go. That's it. Seriously, if you don't know what the TARDIS is, then why are you even reading this book? Vehicle that's bigger inside than out and can travel anywhere through time and space. Though there is so much more to it than that.

A B C D E F G H I J K L M N O P Q R S T U V W X Y Z

Temporal Rift

A hole in time. Not safe, but brimming with Time Energy – and the TARDIS loves that. There's a big Temporal Rift in Cardiff (I know – Cardiff!). So I sometimes just park the TARDIS there for a while when she's a bit low and needs recharging.

Time Energy

Energy that is released when something happens to time itself. Hence Time Energy – see? Very useful, very dangerous. Don't mess with the Time Energy. Leave that to the professionals. Or in extreme cases, me.

Time Lords

The Lords of Time. Ancient and powerful race from the planet Gallifrey that discovered the secrets of time travel many many millions of years ago. Now all gone – except me. I think. Probably. Sadly. There was a big war – the Great Time War – between the Time Lords and the Daleks, though other races and cultures were dragged into it. Nasty. And pretty final. The Daleks were all but wiped out – in fact, everyone thought they were gone forever, including me. The Time Lords really were. With a couple of notable exceptions. I'm the most notable exception there can ever be.

Time Rotor

Quite a useful TARDIS control thing. The Time Rotor is that big glass column in the middle of the TARDIS console that goes up and down when the TARDIS is in flight. Some people seem to think it's actually just a little read-out on the main console. Maybe it was, once. Though actually, I make most of the names up anyway.

Time Vector Generator

Oh, that's another one. TARDIS thingy that's really useful for, you know, stuff. Time stuff. It's what helps to keep the TARDIS bigger inside than outside. But the clever thing is you can also use it as a power booster – I did that once to sort out the Cybermen by increasing the power of an X-ray laser.

Time Vortex

The Time Vortex is that swirly thing the TARDIS travels through. Remember I said the Universe included everything? Well the Time Vortex is one of those bits that it doesn't include, OK? Word of caution – never ever try travelling through the Time Vortex without a TARDIS. Not good.

A B C D E F G H I J K L M N O P Q R S T U V W X Y Z

Time War, the

Known as 'great', but it wasn't all that great. Rather horrible actually – like all wars. Even more nasty than most. The Time Lords foresaw a time when the Daleks would rule the Universe (and probably the Time Vortex too) and they didn't think that was good news at all. So they sent me back to try to stop the Daleks ever being created (ignore that 'Blinovitch Limitation' entry for now, all right?). Didn't work (so maybe you can read up on Blinovitch after all). But the Daleks found out and they were like, livid. Anyway, to cut a long story short – big war. No one won, everyone lost. Daleks are almost wiped out and I'm the Last of the Time Lords. End of. Literally.

Timey-wimey

Anything to do with time can be timey-wimey in a wibbly-wobbly sort of way. It's all rather tricky for a little human mind to cope with, so calling it timey-wimey makes it sound more sort of cosy and easy and sensible, don't you think?

Time Winds

You know I said don't go out in the Time Vortex without a TARDIS? Well that's partly because of the Time Winds. They're not like ordinary winds. The Time Winds breathe on you, and that's it – aged to extinction. When you were a child someone once told you, 'Don't pull that face in case the wind changes' because you'd be stuck like that forever. If the Time Wind changes, then that's even worse. So, if in doubt, don't pull faces.

Untempered Schism, the

There is a theory that all Time Lord power came from the Untempered Schism. Well, maybe not all Time Lord power, but things like the ability to regenerate and all that sort of thing. It's a rip in the fabric of space and time. You can look through it into the Time Vortex itself. I wouldn't recommend it though – not pleasant. Time Lords have to do it as part of our training. It affects different people in different ways – it inspires some, scares others. It drove the Master mad. Me? I just wanted to run away from it, which I think is a pretty healthy response, all things considered.

Total Event Collapse

Now this is the biggie. Like the Big Bang, only backwards. No, not backwards, not like the Great Crunch. Worse than that. And quicker. It takes a huge, catastrophic event to trigger a Total Event Collapse – like a TARDIS exploding or worse. If there is worse. Every sun becomes a supernova at every point in history, and the Universe itself will never have existed. Pretty serious stuff. Best avoided.

Science and Technology Things

On the Clever-Clever scale some of this is right up there with Wort Fangler's Theory of Hydroponic Evolution. So pay attention. There might be a test. Not an exam sort of test or anything like that, but the sort of test where you need to know this stuff or you die. That sort of test. So no pressure.

Android

There are robots and then there are robots. Androids are robots, but robots that look human. Well, maybe not completely human, not always. On Androzani Minor, Sharaz Jek built himself some basic arms-and-legs-and-head things. But then again on Tara they looked as human as human can be. Or as Taran as Taran can be. And the Kraals used androids to replace real people when they tried to invade Earth. Even made copies of me and Sarah Jane. Cheek.

Antimatter

Ah, now here it gets a bit technical. Antimatter is like the opposite of matter. Tricky stuff – because if it ever comes into contact with matter then there's a big explosion as they sort of cancel each other out. So, difficult to study it really. Matter is just 'stuff' so antimatter is just 'not-stuff'. OK?

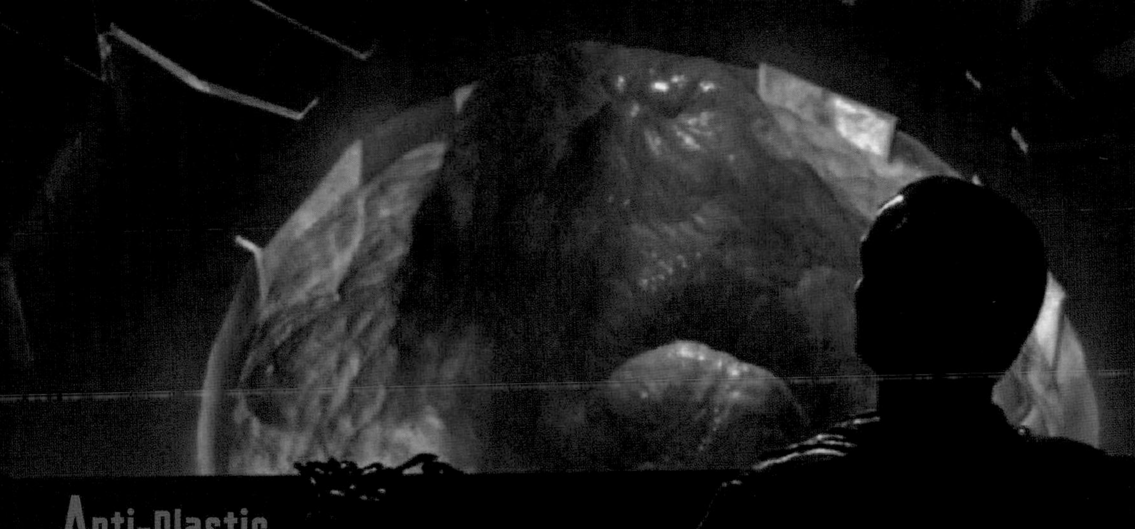

Anti-Plastic

No, not the opposite of plastic. But they do cancel out like matter and anti-matter. Anti-Plastic destroys plastic. Which can be rather dangerous, if you think of that plastic-eaters incident way back in the 1970s. But used properly anti-plastic can be very useful. Like for destroying bits and pieces of the Nestene Consciousness if it gets out of hand.

Apollo 11

You humans – such endeavour! *Apollo 11* was the first manned mission to the Moon back in 1969. Or is it forward? Depends when you're reading this, I suppose. Anyway, there were several *Apollo* missions using big rockets – I mean, really big. And *Apollos 11*, *12*, and *14* to *17* went to the Moon. *13* was supposed to but got into a bit of trouble and never got there. It worked out all right in the end though.

A
B
C
D
E
F
G
H
I
J
K
L
M
N
O
P
Q
R
S
T
U
V
W
X
Y
Z

Atmos

Clever car computer sat-nav thing which also cut car emissions to zero, developed by Luke Rattigan. Except it wasn't because the Sontarans gave him the technology. They used ATMOS as part of their plan to turn Earth into a Sontaran Clone World. Cars as weapons – that's sneaky. And nasty.

Block Transfer Computation

Maths is more powerful than you think. Just by the power of sums and computations of numbers you can create whole realities. That's Block Transfer Computation. The Logopolitans use it a lot, and they have to do all the sums in their heads and chant the answers because otherwise the calculations would affect the computer that was doing them. Only the living mind is immune. Neat stuff.

Chameleon Arch

Pretty whizzo Time Lord stuff this. I've used it myself. Basically it's a way of hiding. You know how if you're really scared by something on the television and you go and hide behind the sofa? Well, it's nothing at all like that. This hides you from yourself. It conceals your real identity and memories and everything and puts them safe and sound somewhere that isn't inside your head – like a pocket watch, for example. Then you can get them back later. If you remember that you even had them, or where you put them. So, a few drawbacks, but still pretty cool stuff.

Clone

A clone is a copy, an exact replica – simple as that. So when you clone a living cell, you make a copy of it. Clone all the cells in someone's body and you have a copy of them. Probably as a baby (or even younger) and then they need to grow up. Some races actually reproduce by cloning – the Sontarans for example, they're all clones. All identical, though that doesn't mean they're all the same. If you see what I mean. They can clone other people too – as they are now. They did that to Martha Jones, poor girl.

Computer

I have a love-hate relationship with computers. Not really fond of them as such, but they can be useful. They're just jumped-up adding machines really. Good at sums. Not so good when they go all wobbly and decide to take over the company (like BOSS) or the world (like WOTAN) or the Universe… There are exceptions, of course. Xoanon was a computer that thought it was me. So at least it had good taste.

Cryogenics

Freezing. That's it, pretty much. It's all about freezing things for later. But not like oven chips or pizza. We're talking about freezing people. So, if you've got this disease and you don't happen to be a Time Lord who can regenerate out of it, then you might have yourself cryogenically frozen and then woken up once they've found a cure. Or not. It's useful for any sort of long wait if you don't have a TARDIS and can't just nip forward in time – long space flights, or waiting for your planet to cool down again after solar flares scorch its surface. That sort of thing.

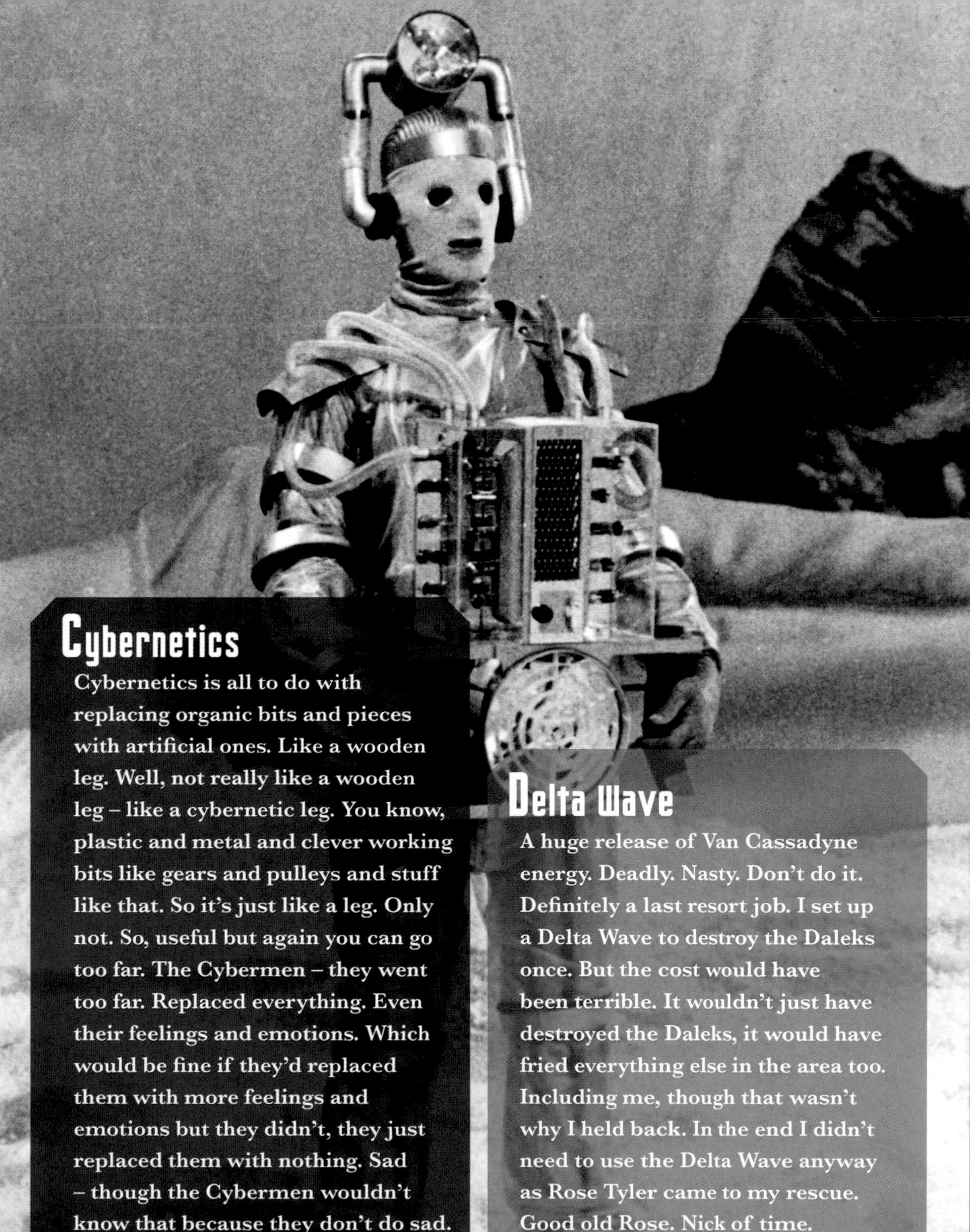

Cybernetics

Cybernetics is all to do with replacing organic bits and pieces with artificial ones. Like a wooden leg. Well, not really like a wooden leg – like a cybernetic leg. You know, plastic and metal and clever working bits like gears and pulleys and stuff like that. So it's just like a leg. Only not. So, useful but again you can go too far. The Cybermen – they went too far. Replaced everything. Even their feelings and emotions. Which would be fine if they'd replaced them with more feelings and emotions but they didn't, they just replaced them with nothing. Sad – though the Cybermen wouldn't know that because they don't do sad.

Delta Wave

A huge release of Van Cassadyne energy. Deadly. Nasty. Don't do it. Definitely a last resort job. I set up a Delta Wave to destroy the Daleks once. But the cost would have been terrible. It wouldn't just have destroyed the Daleks, it would have fried everything else in the area too. Including me, though that wasn't why I held back. In the end I didn't need to use the Delta Wave anyway as Rose Tyler came to my rescue. Good old Rose. Nick of time.

Dalekanium

The metal that Dalek casings are made from. It's very tough, obviously. Keeps them safe inside in their little world of hate and anger. It also conducts gamma radiation quite nicely, but that's not really important. Well, not usually.

DNA

DeoxyriboNucleic Acid to you and me. Well, to scientists anyway. The building stuff of life itself. It's the stuff that contains the genetic instructions that make an individual, well, individual. Don't mess with it. (You listening, Professor Lazarus?)

Dwarf Star Alloy

Didn't we do this? I think we did this. But it's really tough stuff, a metal alloy forged from the stuff dwarf stars are made from (well – duh – given it's called Dwarf Star Alloy that's pretty obvious). Anyhow, it's pretty strong, very heavy, and can even keep a time sensitive like a Tharil chained to the same timeline.

$E=MC^2$

Oh, everyone knows that. Not so many know what it means – which is that energy is equal to mass times the speed of light squared. Which in turn means that the speed of light is a limiting factor – you just can't go faster than light. Well, faster than the speed of light in a vacuum because light slows down in stuff like water and glass... So there you go – easy. Wrong, but easy.

$E=MC^3$

Ah now you're talking – this is how the same thing works in the extra-dimensional physics of the Time Vortex. Double easy.

Eye-Drive

It might sound like someone offering to give you a lift, but actually an eye-drive is one of those eye patch things. Really neat, except when they get hacked – that's not so good. Anyway, they're a way of making sure you remember the Silence. Do you remember the Silence? You're probably wearing an eye-drive then.

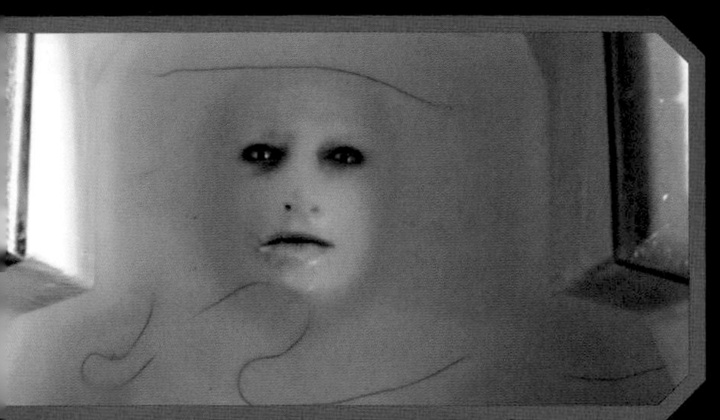

Flesh, the

Gloopy goo-goo stuff that's all slurpy-wurpy. But the clever thing is that you can build things out of it. Not just things – people. A bit like clones. But not really. They call them 'Gangers' which is short for doppelgängers – which means doubles. So the Flesh Ganger has the memories and skills and talents of the original. Sometimes it even thinks it is the original – like when the Silence and Madame Kovarian made a Flesh copy of Amy Pond. Still not happy about that, actually…

Gadget

Well, a gadget is a gadget, isn't it? Except this Gadget – this particular gadget (with a capital 'G') was a robot on Bowie Base One on Mars. Very useful. Got us all out of a lot of trouble. Gadget was remote-controlled and could whizz about on little tracks, very clever. And he had loads of, well – gadgets. Don't know how he got his name.

A B C D E F G H I J K L M N O P Q R S T U V W X Y Z

Genesis Ark, the

This one had me confused for a while. Until I realised it was actually something the Daleks had stolen from the Time Lords during the Great Time War. Their problem was they couldn't open it. Not without my help, or the help of another time traveller. Thank you, Mickey Smith – nice one. Not really his fault though, to be fair. Anyway, where were we? Oh yes – Time Lord technology, so it was bigger inside than outside, like a TARDIS. And the Genesis Ark was a prison – full of captured Daleks. So when it opened up over London – Big Trouble (with capital letters).

Genetic Manipulation Device

Actually it was a sonic micro-field manipulator. Used hyposonic sound waves. But let's not split hairs. Or DNA strands – which is what this thing did. Invented by Professor Lazarus, who was naïve enough to use it on himself. He thought he'd turned younger, but actually he'd turned monster. Not nice.

Gravity Bubble

Now it depends what you're talking about here, doesn't it? Because that chap Bracewell (though he wasn't a chap, he was a robot made by the Daleks), he 'invented' a gravity bubble that enabled Spitfires to fly in space. How cool is that? But a Gravity Bubble is also the thing you get if a TARDIS lands inside another TARDIS – dimensional recursion. The first TARDIS is inside the second TARDIS, which is itself inside the first TARDIS and so on and so on for ever and ever. Now that really is confusing. So make your mind up which Gravity Bubble you mean.

Gravity Well

Now that's just a posh way of talking about a pit. A hole. OK, if you like – a well. Usually down the middle of a spaceship to provide access to the crystal nucleus of a stardrive space engine. Pompous, but handy.

Hallucinogenic Lipstick

Never ever ever – and I mean this – ever kiss River Song. Not ever. Well, you probably wouldn't anyway. But if you would then, you know, don't. Ever. Because she doesn't wear lipstick like other girls do, all bright colours and matching eyeshadow. Oh no. River's lippy might be poisoned (tried that once – yuk!), or more likely it'll put you into a hallucino-suggestible state. Which basically means she can tell you whatever she likes and you'll believe her. Actually, looking into her eyes can have a similar effect with no cosmetic enhancements needed. Um, never mind that right now.

Handbot

Robots used on Apalapucia. They're called Handbots because they have hands. Well, that's not as daft as it sounds – they don't have faces, so they can't actually see. No faces – no eyes. Except they can see through their hands. Which are organic. Amy had a rough time on Apalapucia. I was only there briefly, but Amy got stuck in a different timeline and was there for a lifetime. No, really.

A B C D E F G H I J K L M N O P Q R S T U V W X Y Z

Home Box

You've heard of the 'Black Box' in an aircraft? It's not usually black, actually, but never mind. A Home Box is pretty much the same for spaceships. If the ship crashes or explodes or suffers some other catastrophe, then the Home Box heads to the ship's home port with all the flight data. You have to wonder, though – if they can build a special box that will survive a crash or explosion or black hole or whatever, why don't they just make the whole spaceship out of the same material?

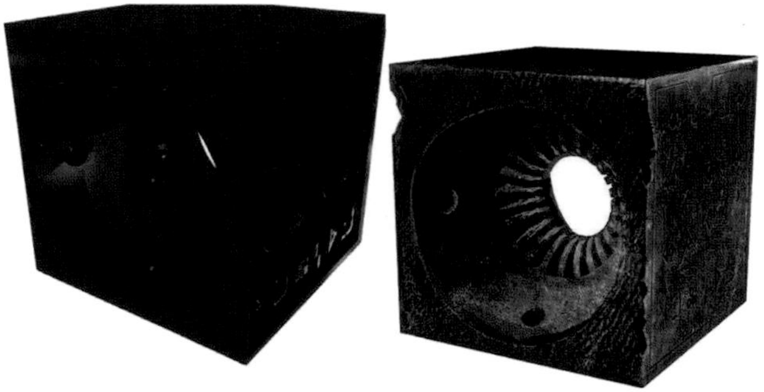

H^2O Scoop

Ah, now this is clever. The Judoon use it sometimes. It's a device that can scoop up (scoop – see?) something, even a whole building, and put it somewhere else. It does affect the weather though. Rain caught up in the field goes upwards.

Immortality Gate

Not, as its name suggests, a way of making people immortal at all. It's a Vinvocci medical device that can treat whole groups of beings suffering from the same sorts of illness and restore them all to health. It takes a biological imprint of the species and uses that as a healthy template. Which is how the Master managed to use one of these to turn the whole human race into versions of himself. Clever, but unpleasant.

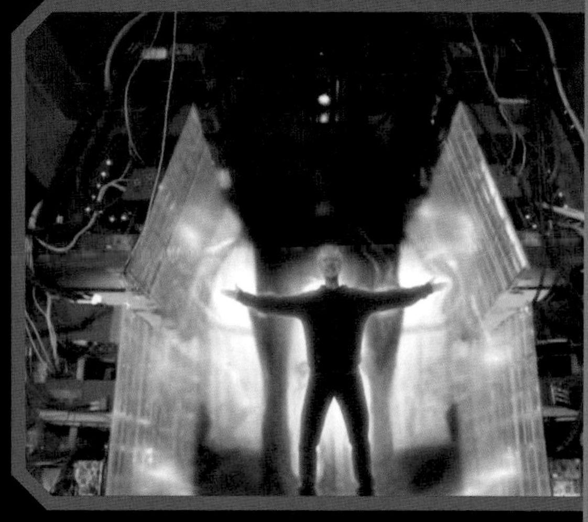

Infostamp

Data storage. Crude and boring. Yawn. Actually, they are a lot more advanced than anything you've got in the 21st century, but even so... The Cybermen use them. Well, that says it all really.

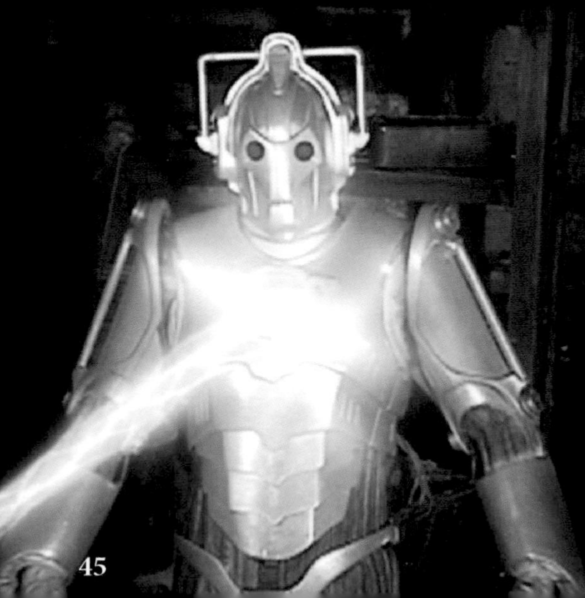

A B C D E F G H I J K L M N O P Q R S T U V W X Y Z

Ironside

That's what Professor Bracewell called the war machine he thought he'd invented during World War 2. Good name. Trouble is, he didn't invent the Ironside at all – it invented him. Because the Ironsides were Daleks, and Bracewell was a robot they'd programmed to think he'd created them.

Key to Time

The Key to Time is one of the most powerful artefacts in known creation. Well, any creation whether it's known or not. It's so powerful it was split into seven pieces, six of which were scattered through time and space and disguised. The seventh piece was the Core of the key which I had to use once to track down the other bits for the White Guardian. He's pretty powerful too, actually. Once assembled the Key is a translucent cube that can restore balance to the Universe. Or seriously unbalance it.

Nanogenes

Tiny little things, nanogenes – really really small. We're talking at the atomic level small, which is small as small can be. They're little robot things that can repair the genetic structure of someone who's injured. Provided they understand that structure – otherwise, big problems, because they get their repairs all wrong. Which can be worse than what you started with – like the Empty Child, and the Gas Mask Zombies... Turned out all right in the end though.

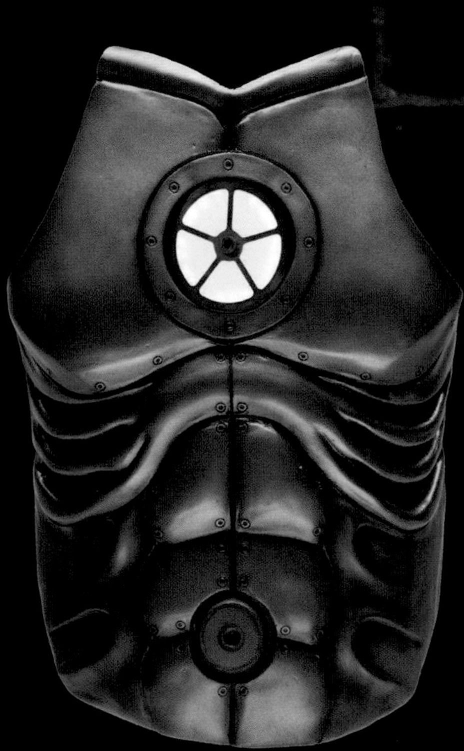

Oblivion Continuum

A small but highly effective power source. Also highly unstable – with a bit of encouragement it can explode. Big Time. The sort of encouragement the Daleks gave to the oblivion continuum that powered the robotic Professor Bracewell.

Paradox Machine

A piece of equipment that makes it possible for time to get all tangled up with itself. That makes it sound simple, which it isn't – you need to adapt a TARDIS or something. Like the Master did when he created a Paradox Machine out of my TARDIS, so that the Toclafane could come back from the future to destroy the human race, which was their own ancestors.

Reality Bomb

Oh this is really nasty. One of Davros's more unpleasant inventions. Though actually most of his inventions are pretty unpleasant – especially the Daleks. It uses Z-Nutrino Energy to cancel out the atoms in reality. Not nice. The good news is you need a huge power source to make it work. The bad news is that being Davros, he got one…

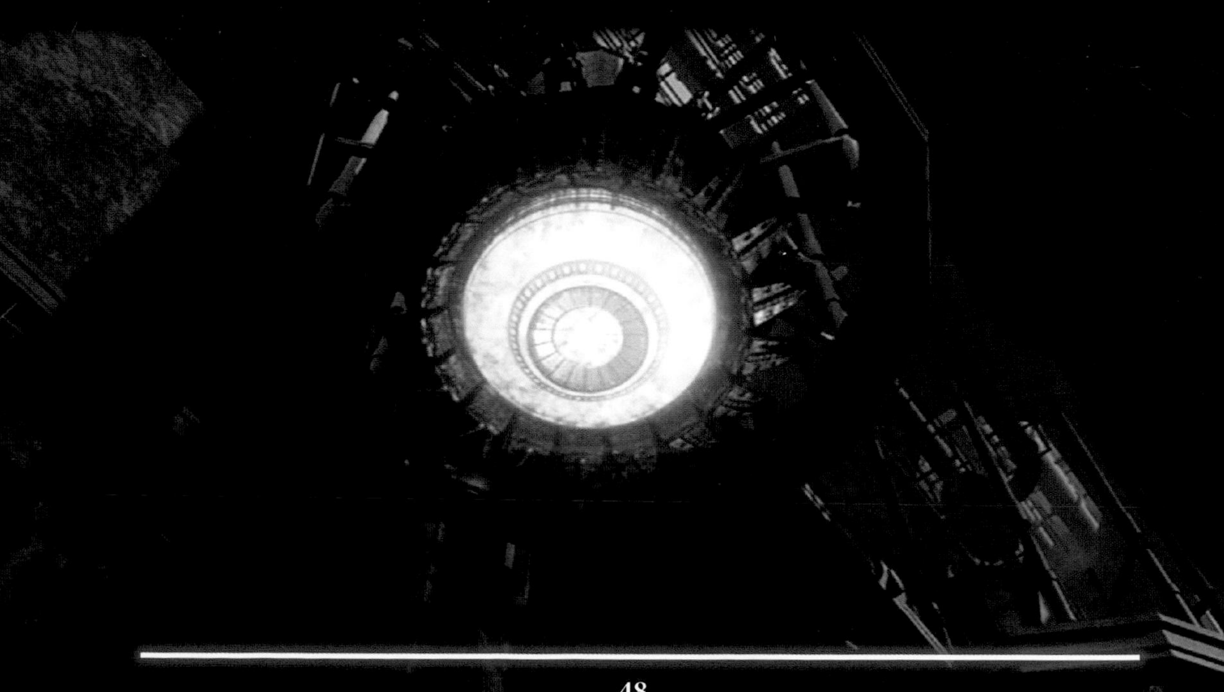

Robot

A robot is really any mechanical apparatus that does work that a human could have done. Like menial tasks such as building cars, right up to more sophisticated tasks like actually thinking about stuff. The word 'robot' comes from the Czech word for 'slave'.

Satellite

A satellite is anything that goes round something else. Like a moon orbiting a planet. Generally when we talk about a satellite we mean an artificial one. It might be quite small, like the satellites that redirect phone calls or send global positioning information. Or it might be a space station in orbit round a planet – like Satellite 5, or Platform One, or Station 3. They don't have to have numbers in their names, but they often do.

Skasis Paradigm, the

The so-called 'God Maker', this is a mathematical equation that enables you to control the basic energies of the universe and everything. Or it would, if you could solve it. Never been done, luckily. Though the Krillitanes came close.

Space pig

Poor thing was actually just a pig. The Slitheen stuck him in a spacesuit and rewired his brain. Then they put him inside a spaceship and flew it into Big Ben before crashing it into the Thames. It was all part of a plan to make you humans think you were being invaded. By pigs from space – I ask you. Gullible lot.

Special Drinking Straw

Best invention ever. It makes fizzy drinks even more fizzy. Get yourself one – seriously.

Speed of Light

Fast. That do? Really really fast. I mean, have a go at turning on a torch and try to see the beam travel out from the torch to hit whatever you're shining it at. The speed of light in a vacuum is about 186,000 miles per second. That's nearly 300 million metres per second.

Stattenheim Remote Control

A remote control for a TARDIS. Amazing, eh? You can summon your TARDIS to any place and time. Even open the doors. I've always wanted one of these. Had one once. For a bit. Had to give it back though. Not happy.

Subwave Network

Well, it's a communications system, that's all. Clever though. Video links, phone connections, the lot. Developed using technology from my friend Mr Copper, and used by Harriet Jones (you know who she is) to keep everyone in touch when the Daleks invaded. Until they killed her. Poor Harriet. We had our disagreements, but I liked her.

Tethered Aerial Release Developed In Style (TARDIS)

Or rather, not a TARDIS. When Jackson Lake thought he was actually the Doctor (long story), he knew he needed a TARDIS to get about the place. So he had one built. Only his TARDIS was a hot air balloon. Still useful for destroying a CyberKing and saving Victorian London from total destruction though.

Telephone

Long-distance talky thing. You know. You must know. I bet you've used one. Invented by Alexander Graham Bell, it originally sent sounds down wires. Now it's all cell networks and wireless and cordless and mobile with texting and everything. And apps – I love apps. They call them SmartPhones, but actually it's the people who use them that are smart. Usually. Well, sometimes.

Teleport

Same as a TransMat, really. We'll get to that in a minute, OK?

Teselecta

Shape-changing, time-travelling robot operated by a miniaturised crew that live inside it. So it can imitate all sorts of people and creatures. The Department used the Teselecta to hunt down criminals who'd escaped justice. Like River Song. Useful thing, though – saved me, I can tell you. When you've got to die at a specific point in space and time and you just can't avoid it, hiding inside a Teselecta is a pretty cool move.

Transmat

Same as a teleport really. Except it doesn't need a receiving station at the other end. So we've covered that now. Moving on…

Vortex Manipulator

Rather basic time travel device. You wear it on the wrist and dial in where you want to go. The ride's not very comfortable – nothing like the luxury of TARDIS travel, I can tell you. But the Time Agency rather likes these. Captain Jack Harkness kept his when he 'left'.

Warp Matrix Engineering

A key Time Lord technology. We experimented with all sorts of things, like Tachyonics and other faster-than-light stuff, before we hit on this. It's how we power TARDISes.

Water Pistol

If you don't have a water pistol, then get one. Now. They are so cool. A gun that's not a gun – more of a water-squirter thing. Useful for defending yourself against Pyrovile-possessed priestesses and that sort of thing. Or just soaking people for fun.

Winders

Partly robotic law-enforcement and maintenance force on *Starship UK*. They used the same technology as the information-robot Smilers. A bit sinister, if I'm honest about it.

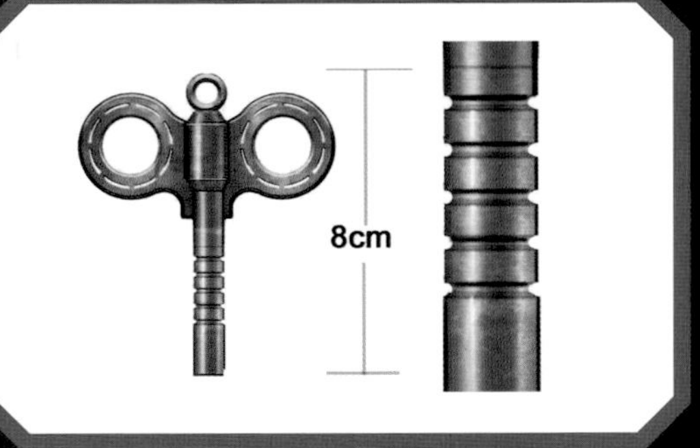

Yo-yo

Even better than a water pistol. OK, a yo-yo might look like a disc on a string, but you can do all sorts of things with it. Not just the let-it-drop down-the-string-and-pull-it-up-again thing, though that's a good start. But you should see my double back loops. Oh, and it's also useful for taking gravity readings.

Zeus plugs

Don't worry about these. You probably won't need them unless you have a TARDIS. And you don't. But if you do, and you need to get at your Zeus Plugs, you'll probably need a Ganymede Driver.

Now Get Out of That

At some point you're going to be locked up, or stuck somewhere, or unable to open a thing – or wanting to lock it shut… So here are some handy bits and pieces that might help with that sort of thing. Might – no guarantees, mind.

Deadlock Seal

Oh, if I had an extra pound for every deadlock seal I've come across, I'd be a lot heavier. It's the one sort of lock that the Sonic Screwdriver just can't open. Well, that and wood – it's not great on wood. But a deadlock seal, that really gives it problems. Anything with a deadlock seal is very, very difficult to open.

Emergency Temporal Shift

Daleks do this sometimes, and it is very annoying. Not just any Dalek, but clever ones like the Cult of Skaro – they can just buzz off to another time and escape. It can be very awkward. I guess the good news is that it uses up a lot of their power, so it really is a last resort.

Osterhagen Key

There are five of these keys. They really are keys, but they unlock a device not a door. The Osterhagen Keys are a last resort – if Earth is invaded, and there really is no hope for the human race, then all five keys can be used in unison to set off a chain of twenty-five nuclear bombs placed below the surface of the planet. You humans really don't do things by halves, do you? I mean – what a daft idea. However bad things are, there's always hope. Always.

Perception Filter

These are great. If you've got a perception filter you can hide in plain sight. People just sort of look away and don't register anything that's protected by a perception filter. If they really know it's there and actually want to see it, then they can. But for hiding something that seems pretty inconsequential anyway – like a pocket watch, or an extra door in Amelia Pond's house – then it's great.

Psychic Paper

My favourite! Well, after the Sonic Screwdriver maybe. The paper's just slightly psychic, just enough to determine what I want people to see, or what they expect to see. Then that's what it shows them. Easy. Great for getting into places. Or out of them. Doesn't always work though as people can be trained to spot it and resist.

Reverse the polarity of the neutron flow

If in doubt, that's what you do. If all else fails, if there's nothing else you can think of, then reverse the polarity of the neutron flow. You'll be surprised how often it works. Or if you're not sure quite what you actually did, just tell them 'I reversed the polarity.' They'll be none the wiser.

Run!

Another 'if in doubt' one. If in doubt – run! Again, you'll be surprised how often it works. If no one chases after you, then maybe it wasn't strictly necessary. But usually you'll find people do run after you. And there's often shooting and stuff. Just so you're warned.

Sonic Screwdriver

Ah, now this really is my favourite. I've had several Sonic Screwdrivers – they often get broken or lost or given away at Christmas (well, not really) so I have to build a newer, better model. It's improving all the time. It's sonic, and it's a screwdriver – what's not to like?

Stormcage Containment Facility

Basically, a prison. Maximum security, escape-proof, totally secure. Unless you're River Song, of course – then you can just walk out pretty much whenever you want. But no one else can get out. And if they did, the weather outside is rubbish anyway.

Time Paradox

That's when time gets all muddled up and goes wrong. There's a thing called the Grandfather Paradox about what happens and how muddled things would get if you went back in time and killed your own grandfather before he had any children. Not that you'd do that – it would be so daft. But, basically, don't mess with time. Not unless you're an expert, like me.

Nice and Helpful 'People'

There are some lovely helpful people – by which I mean 'people' if you know what I mean – in the universe. But if you need someone you can depend on and trust – then here's a few people ('people') who have been good to me in the past. And the present. And indeed the future.

Arwell family, the

Lovely bunch. There was a bit of trouble, as there so often is. Madge helped me when I fell out of a spaceship, so it seemed only right to return the favour. Her husband Reg was missing in action during the war – he flew a Lancaster Bomber and got lost coming home one moonless night. But Madge and the children, Lily and Cyril, helped me organise an escape for some tree spirits. Long story, but it all ended happily. Reg was home for Christmas, just like he'd promised.

Avery, Captain Henry

Seventeenth century English pirate with, I have to say, an impressive beard. I met him after his ship was becalmed and he started losing his crew to a mysterious Siren. One small cut was enough for the Siren to latch on to someone and attack. Except she wasn't really attacking, but that's another story…

Boe, the Face of

The oldest living creature of the Isop galaxy, and the last of his kind. I was there when he died – it was so sad. He gave his life so that people trapped in an enclosed motorway on New Earth could escape. It was said the sky would split open when he died, and as the tunnel roof slid back, I guess that's what happened.

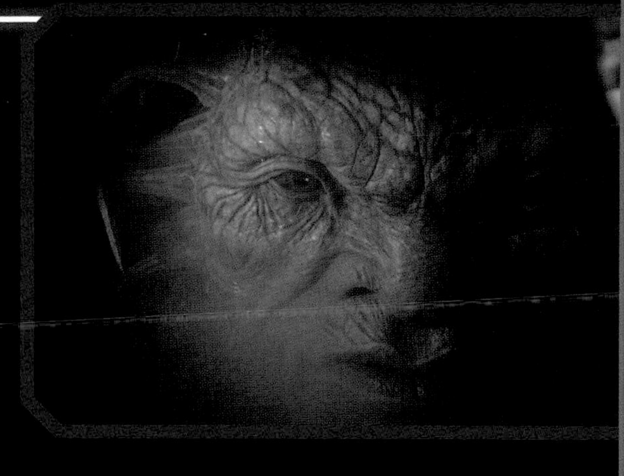

Cheem, the Forest of

Cheem is a lovely planet. Very woody. Lots of woods. And the Forest of Cheem – living trees, how cool is that? I met a few of them on Platform One, when we watched the End of the World. Lovely people. But be careful when you shake hands – you might get splinters.

A B C D E F G H I J K L M N O P Q R S T U V W X Y Z

Christie, Agatha

What a charming and clever lady. You probably know her as the writer of all those really amazing detective stories where you get to the end and find out whodunnit and think: 'Of course, I should have realised'. I remember her for that business with Donna Noble and the giant wasp...

Churchill, Winston

Winston is great. A bit set in his ways, rather single-minded, but great. We've helped each other out so many times. There was that business in World War 2 with the Daleks, and then that time when time stopped. So it wasn't a time at all really... Anyway, wartime British prime minister who led Britain through the Blitz and on to victory. Top chap.

Cleopatra

Now be careful. Because you might think you're meeting a famous personage from history, like this legendary queen of Egypt. Then it turns out to be River Song all dolled up and making the most of her hallucinogenic lipstick. So watch out for that.

Delaware III, Canton Everett

Canton was a big help getting President Nixon to understand about the Silence back in the late 1960s. We had a few tense moments together, and I had to explain to him about mobile phones. Worked for the FBI, until he was sacked. Then reinstated. Then possibly sacked again, I lose track rather. It was nice to have him there over forty years later when I 'died' at Lake Silencio.

Dickens, Charles

Top writer. Very big in his day, which was in the 19th century, and ever since actually. I met him in Cardiff. At Christmas. He was doing a reading of one of his stories, I was battling against a ghostly ethereal life form called the Gelth. We hooked up, sorted out the problem, went our separate ways. But he's great – I'm a fan.

van Gogh, Vincent

There's no one like Vincent. Never has been, never will be. Poor chap – very troubled. Such a fantastic painter, but never recognised while he was alive. I'm just glad that once we'd sorted out some of his demons – in the form of an invisible, blind monster Krafayis – Amy and I were able to show him just how great and valued he would become...

A B C D E F G H I J K L M N O P Q R S T U V W X Y Z

Harkness, Captain Jack

You must know Captain Jack. Everyone knows Captain Jack Harkness. That's not his real name, of course. I'm not sure if he remembers his real name. He used to work for the Time Agency – who are a shady lot – but they wiped his memories when he left. Now he runs Torchwood. Oh, and he's immortal too, thanks to that business with Rose Tyler and the Time Vortex. He did tell me once that he's also known as 'the Face of Boe'. But I think he was joking. Maybe. Wasn't he?

Jenny

My daughter Jenny. You didn't know I had a family? Got a granddaughter called Susan too. Though Jenny's not really my daughter. She was created on the planet Messaline out of a sample of my DNA. Died there too, poor thing. As far as I know. Such a pity – she'd have loved to have adventures of her own.

Jones, Harriet MP / PM

You know who she is. Member of Parliament, and then after she helped me sort out the Slitheen, she became Prime Minister. Sorted out the Sycorax – a little too comprehensively for my liking. She was getting carried away, so I had to do something about that. Not proud of it, but it had to be done. I think she understood. She helped us all again – against the Daleks when they invaded. They exterminated her for it though.

Jones, Martha

Martha was such a good friend. I took her to New Earth, and to meet Shakespeare, and all sorts of places. She sorted out the Master and the Toclafane – I knew she would. But it took its toll. I did see her again a couple of times, like when she asked me to help her get rid of the Sontarans. Eventually she met up with Mickey Smith and the rest, as they say, is history. Why do they say that, do you suppose?

K-9

My dog! And what a dog. A robot dog. He's got a nose laser and ear-sensors. I don't mean he can sense ears, that wouldn't be very useful – his ears are sensors. Neat, eh? K-9 travelled with me in the TARDIS, in various forms, for a long time. But now he lives with Sarah Jane Smith and helps her out. Lovely Sarah Jane.

Lake, Jackson

Did I ever tell you about how I met a version of myself from the future? Actually, I've done that a few times. But this one time – at Christmas, again – was really confusing. Because it wasn't me at all. It was Jackson Lake. But he thought he was me, because he'd absorbed my memories from a Cyberman Infostamp. He had a lovely companion, just like I do. A neat screwdriver – though not sonic. And even a TARDIS, though that was a bit different from mine.

Lethbridge-Stewart, Brigadier

What can I say about the Brigadier? He was a lowly colonel when we first met – way back in my second incarnation. But we became such good friends. Didn't always see eye to eye when I worked for him. Well, that's what he thought. I don't work for anyone, but I deigned to give UNIT the benefit of my expertise for a while. Well, I was exiled to 20th-century Earth so I didn't have much choice. There will never be anyone quite like the Brigadier. I do miss him.

Liz Ten

She's only the blooming queen! Liz Ten – Queen Elizabeth the Tenth of *Starship UK*. Though even she didn't know the truth about it – about how the whole huge ship was riding on the back of a Star Whale…

STARSHIP UK

YOU HAVE
CHOSEN TO
FORGET.
GO IN PEACE.

Maldovar, Dorium

Ran a bar that was humbly called The Maldovarium – the sort of place where you could get anything, for a price. And people did. He owed me a few favours, and helped at Demon's Run. Though he lost his head. Literally. The Headless Monks took it and put it in a box. That didn't slow him down much though – he was still a useful source of information. When he was in a helpful mood.

Mott, Wilfred

Donna's granddad. What a gentleman. Didn't know who he was when we first met, but we became firm friends. Every life is worthwhile, every single one. But if you've got to sacrifice yourself for someone else, then to do it for someone like Wilf... Well, that's a privilege.

Noble, Donna

Poor Donna. The first time I saw her she was in her wedding dress and about to get married. One of the last times I saw her she was in her wedding dress and had just got married. But we had such fun in between. I wasn't sure she'd enjoyed our first meeting, but she tracked me down again afterwards and pretty much forced me to take her away on adventures. Which made it all the sadder when I had to erase her memories of all the time we'd spent together. Poor Donna.

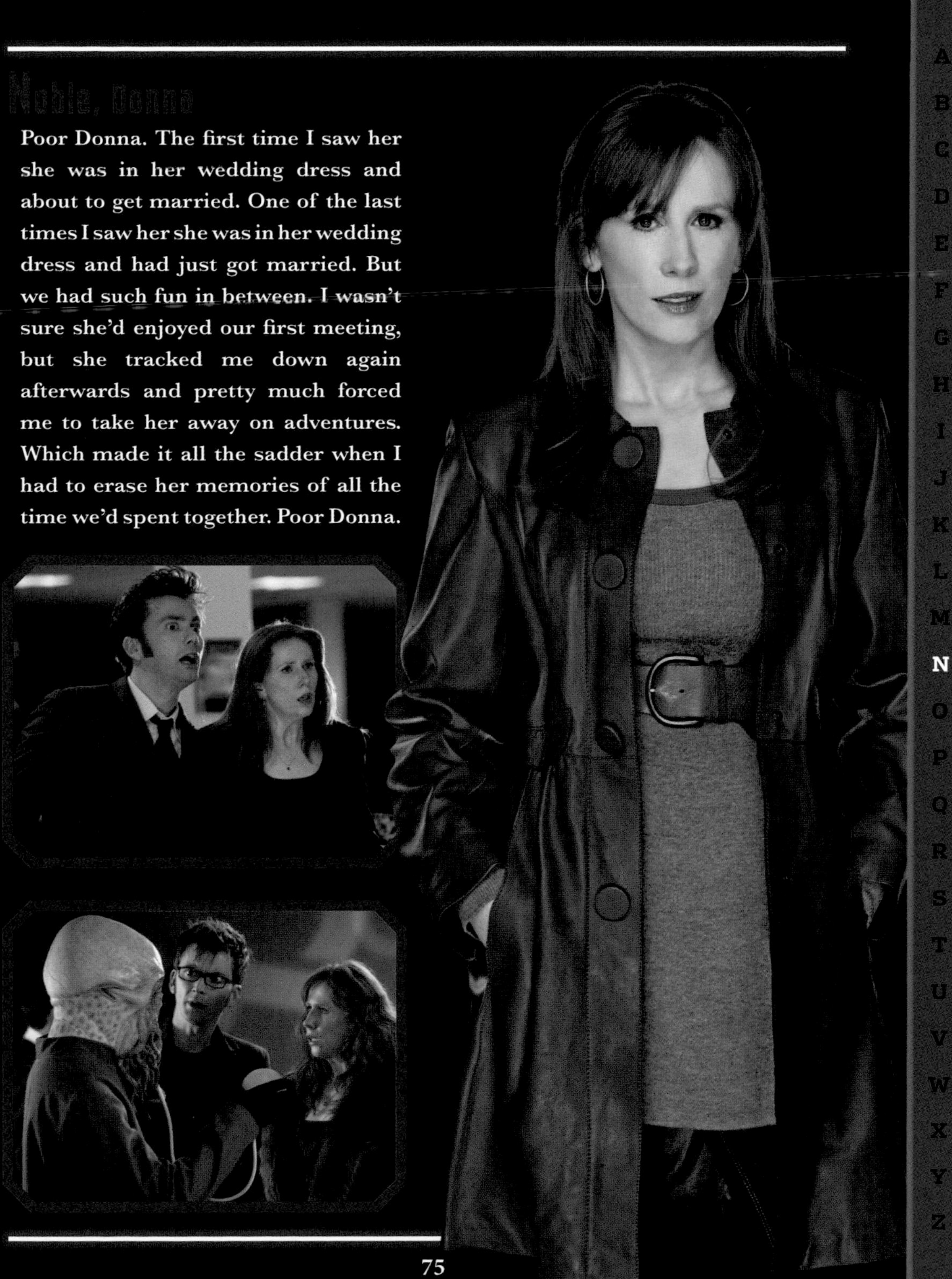

Owens, Craig

Oh, I love Craig. He's my mate. In the matey human sort of sense that is. I was his lodger, you know. I think we got on. He never guessed I wasn't, you know, human. Well, not for days anyway. I helped him and his missus get together. Went back and visited, saw their son – bit miffed they didn't name him after me, but hey, you can't have everything. Oh, and we sorted out some Cybermen too, me and Craig.

Peth, Astrid

I met Astrid on the starship *Titanic* – not an auspicious name for a ship of any kind. I should have guessed what was coming. She was working as a waitress in a cocktail bar, that much is true. But she always knew she'd find a much better place – with or without me. She dreamed of being out among the stars. As things ended up, she's among the stars now, though not quite in the way she imagined. Which is sad.

Pettigrew, Abigail

When Abigail got ill, her family sent her to Kazran Sardick's father, who cryogenically froze her. She was the security for a loan to the family, but they hoped that while she was frozen a cure would be found. She only had a few days to live, and I'm afraid we used them up – young Kazran and me. We defrosted Abigail so she could come out to play, and she never told us. She should have told us. But poor Abigail lived so much in those last days.

Pond, Amy

Where do we start when explaining Amy? The little girl who waited and waited until she wasn't so little any more. Dear, dear Amy – and Rory too (though we'll come to him). She had such a joy, such a love of adventure. I was so sorry to leave her, and so sorry she thought I was gone forever. We had so many good times, so many great adventures together.

Pope, Elton

Elton was on the very edge of my life for a long time. Looking for the Doctor, because he once caught a glimpse of me, and he thought I knew something about the death of his mother. Which I'm afraid I did. Elton was a founder member of LINDA (look it up – near the end), and he was the only real survivor of the group after Victor Kennedy's arrival...

Redfern, Joan

Matron at Farringham School, Joan was unlucky enough to fall in love with John Smith, the History teacher. I say 'unlucky' because John Smith wasn't John Smith at all. It was me. But I didn't know that – I really and truly thought I was John Smith. I thought I was human, and you know what? I fell in love with Joan too. But that was when I was someone else, and it was all very sad. Except when it was very wonderful.

Reinette

When I first met Reinette she was a little girl. But she grew up quickly – very quickly from where I was looking – and became the famous French lady Madame de Pompadour. I kept popping into her life at different stages as I tried to find out what was going on with this spaceship that had windows that opened on to different times in Reinette's history. The ship's clockwork repair robots were after Reinette's head, hoping it could somehow help them fix the ship. No idea what that was all about. But I saved her. At least, I saved her from the robots.

Sardick, Kazran

Businessman, money-lender, generally sour old man. But I knew him when he was younger too. Played with him when he was a boy. We did lots together – me and Kazran and Abigail. And eventually he did get back his sense of perspective, and his joy of life. Eventually.

A B C D E F G H I J K L M N O P Q R S T U V W X Y Z

Saxon, Lucy

The Master's wife. Yeah – you did read that correctly. The Master's wife. Not a very rewarding job, I'd have thought. And sure enough, she shot him. And then she did all she could to stop him from ever coming back.

Shakespeare, William

Only the greatest poet and playwright the human race has ever produced. Some people find him a bit boring or difficult when they're younger – they need to try him again. Really. Martha Jones and I met him you know. Nice enough, though a bit full of himself. But I suppose that's understandable. Together we fought off the Carrionites.

Smith, Mickey

Mickey the Idiot. Except he wasn't an idiot at all. Mickey the clever, resourceful, and when it comes to it, very brave. He and Rose Tyler were great friends, and they both travelled in the TARDIS for a bit. Mickey took time out to live in a parallel world, but then again so did Rose (though against her better judgement). Ended up with Martha Jones – a good match, if you ask me.

Smith, Sarah Jane

How can anyone possibly describe Sarah Jane Smith and do her justice? I'm tempted just to leave it at that. But Sarah Jane, investigative journalist, bravest of the brave, my best friend. So clever, so thoughtful, so feeling. I'd never have let her leave me if she didn't have to. And I left it far too long before I saw her again. My Sarah Jane. How I miss her.

Song, River

You know how I said Sarah was special and unique just now? Well, so is River – but in a completely different way. I saw her as a baby. I was there when she died. I was there when she murdered me, and when she saved my life. I even married her. Well, there were some technical issues with the actual wedding – like the bit where I tell the bride my real name. But it's the thought that counts!

Sparrow, Sally

I hardly knew Sally Sparrow, but she saved me. She had this whole adventure with the Weeping Angels that I guided her through. Then she made notes about it and gave them to me so that when I needed her, I could guide her through. You following me? If not, then look up 'Time Paradox' and see if that helps at all. It probably won't.

de Souza, Lady Christina

A thief. Though she's a good thief – in the sense that she is good at it, not that it's a good thing to do. She just happened to be on a bus I caught. A bus that travelled through a wormhole to another planet where we had to work together, helped by some giant flies, to open the wormhole again and escape back to Earth before the flying stingrays got us. You with me? Then she stole the bus and flew off in it.

Stormageddon

Craig and Sophie Owen's son is really called Alfie. Well, that's what they called him. But because I speak Baby (fluently) I know he reckons he's really Stormageddon, Dark Lord of All. He'll grow out of it. He did for the Cybermen though – Craig sorted them out when he heard Alfie crying. It's amazing what a bit of love can achieve.

Tyler, Jackie

Rose's mum has got a heart of gold, but ooh, she can be hard work sometimes. She slapped me – just for taking Rose away in the TARDIS. OK, so we were gone for a year, but that was an accident. We got on a bit better after she helped battle the Slitheen and actually – don't tell her – she's been a big help on a few occasions. She lives with an alternative version of Rose's dad Pete in another universe now. Probably just as well.

Tyler, Pete

Rose's dad died when she was a baby. But she met him again – by going back in time (not recommended, actually) and in an alternative universe where he never died. Pete helped us against the Cybermen and later against the Daleks too. And then Rose and her mum ended up back on Pete's World with him.

Tyler, Rose

I met Rose when I blew up her job. I was actually trying to stop the Nestene Consciousness invading at the time, but even so I guess she thought it was a bit drastic. We met when I needed her most. I needed someone after the Time War, someone to help me see that life was worth living again, to help me appreciate the marvels of the universe. And that was Rose – no one else could have done it, not as well as she did. It was a terrible moment when we were wrenched apart. I owe her so much.

Vastra, Madame

Silurian crime fighter in Victorian London. Has a sword, ate Jack the Ripper. What more do you really need to know?

Victoria, Queen

And talking of Victorian, here's the lady the Victorians are named after. She gave me a knighthood, you know. But she also set up Torchwood to hunt me down. So, good and bad. She blamed me and Rose for the fact she had trouble with a werewolf, but we saved her from it. I think.

Williams, Rory

Or Mr Pond as I quite often think of him. Amy's husband, and River Song's father – though we won't go into that. He's so devoted, though he can be a bit slow on the uptake sometimes. He died when the crack in time touched him and ripped him out of existence. Even Amy forgot he ever existed. But then he was recreated from her memories as an Auton. Such a human Auton – he'd have waited for Amy forever. Luckily, the universe got rebooted, and Rory was Rory again.

Not So Nice 'People', and Aliens and Monsters and Things

Right, now these are the ones not to go and ask for help. I won't say 'not under any circumstances' because I guess there are always exceptions. Sometimes. Occasionally. Well, I did get help from a Dalek once, but it had been infected with the Human Factor and just wanted to play trains, which was a bit weird if we're honest about it. But rule of thumb (and fingers and hand and arm and everything really) is: Don't.

Abzorbaloff

Nasty green gentleman from the planet Clom. That is, he pretended to be a gentleman called Victor Kennedy. Actually he was, well, green. And absorbed people – nasty. He infiltrated that LINDA lot to try and track me down and absorb me too.

Autons

The Nestene Consciousness can animate anything made of plastic. Its key weapon is the Autons – faceless shop window dummies that have blaster guns hidden inside their hands. But watch out because the Nestenes can also make copies of people that look pretty much like the real thing. Is your best friend an Auton? Think about retrometabalisation... Well, the process is nothing at all like that.

Beast, the

An evil creature, imprisoned even before our universe began by the Disciples of Light. They held it captive on a planet called Krop Tor which circled a black hole. If the Beast ever escaped, then the planet would fall into the Black Hole and destroy it. They hoped. Didn't work out quite like that, I have to say…

Carrionites

Space witches, basically. Not very nice, so they were cast out into the Deep Darkness by the Eternals. Three of them managed to get to Elizabethan London, feeding on the grief and despair of William Shakespeare after the death of his son. They planned to harness the power of his words to open a way for the rest of the Carrionites to return to our universe.

Capricorn, Max

Owned a whole fleet of cruise-liner spaceships. Except his business was in trouble. He had this really neat plan to save it – except that the plan involved destroying one of his ships, the *Titanic*, and killing everyone on-board. Oh, and crashing it into Earth and killing loads of people there too. So, not good. Very not good. Max himself was just a head really, in a mobile life-support system.

Clockwork Robots

Nastiest Clockwork Robots I ever met were really only trying to help. They were supposed to repair a spaceship if it got damaged. But no one told them they shouldn't use bits of the crew to do it. Then they went after the head of Madame de Pompadour in 18th-century France – even opened up time windows to find her. Goodness only knows why they thought that would help.

Cult of Skaro, the

I thought this lot were just a rumour, a legend. Until I met them. The Cult of Skaro – a group of four Daleks who were ordered by the Emperor Dalek to think the unthinkable, to do whatever it took to win the Great Time War. They even had names – Daleks with names. Thay, Caan, Jast, and their leader, Dalek Sec.

Cybermen

People are never satisfied with what they've got, are they? Not that the Cybermen would know that. But they used to be human, except they wanted to be better than human. So they replaced bits and pieces of their bodies, they enhanced their brains, until they were unfeeling creatures of metal and plastic driven by logic rather than emotion. Their one goal is to survive – at any cost.

Cyber Controller

The ultimate leader of the Cybermen is the Cyber Controller. In the alternative universe where the Cybermen were created by John Lumic, he became their first Controller. In our universe it was all a bit different, but that's another story. But in both cases the Cyber Controller has an enlarged brain casing. For his big brain, I guess.

Cyberleader

The Cybermen are organised rather like an army. They have lieutenants and they have Cyberleaders who are responsible for a whole gang of Cybermen. They don't actually call it a 'gang', it's just however many there are to complete whatever it is they're trying to do. The Cyberleader usually has dark markings on the head so you can pick him out. And avoid him.

CyberKing

Not actually a king. But king-sized. A dreadnaught-class Cybership, which is a huge walking, fighting factory to produce more Cybermen. I battled against one in Victorian London – made out of whatever bits and pieces of Victorian technology the stranded Cybermen there could find.

Cybermat

Imagine a metal cybernetic rat. Well a Cybermat isn't much like that. It's bigger and a different shape. More like a silver fish – though a very big one. The Cybermen use them for all sorts of things, like infiltration. They home in on your brain waves, and some of them have very nasty teeth.

Cybershade

Bit of a weird one. This was back in Victorian London, and the Cybermen needed some reinforcements. They didn't have to be very clever, just perform fairly menial tasks. So they made Cybershades out of, well, whatever they could find. Animals, mostly. Like cats and dogs and – yes – probably rats.

Dalek

I think you know what a Dalek is. Everyone knows what a Dalek is. A living, bubbling lump of hate housed inside an armoured life-support system. The only thing a Dalek ever feels is hate, the only thing it ever does is destroy. It's so afraid of everything else that it won't rest until every possible threat has been exterminated. And everything in the universe is a potential threat. Especially me.

Davros

Long, long ago on the planet Skaro, the Thals and the Kaleds waged terrible war for a thousand years. Davros was a Kaled scientist, brilliant but crippled in the war. He realised his people were mutating because of the chemical, nuclear and biological weapons that had been used. He created a life-support system and travel machine for the creatures the Kaleds would become. But then he altered the genetic make-up of those creatures – and created the Daleks.

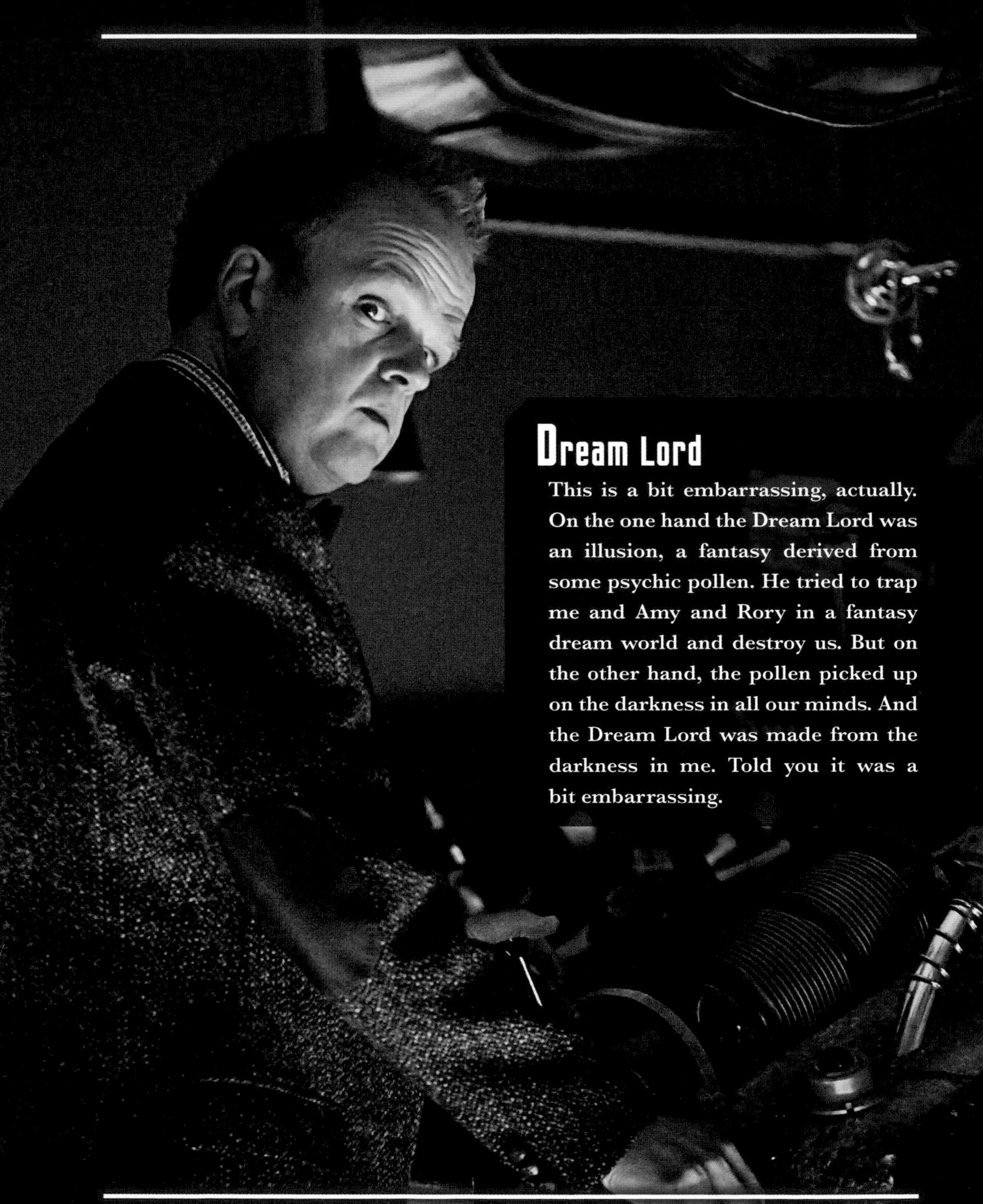

Dream Lord

This is a bit embarrassing, actually. On the one hand the Dream Lord was an illusion, a fantasy derived from some psychic pollen. He tried to trap me and Amy and Rory in a fantasy dream world and destroy us. But on the other hand, the pollen picked up on the darkness in all our minds. And the Dream Lord was made from the darkness in me. Told you it was a bit embarrassing.

Emperor Dalek

The ultimate leader of the Daleks. There have been several Emperors. I've destroyed most of them. One turned out to be Davros, which was a surprise. One gave himself a promotion and thought he was the god of all Daleks. Another one tried to turn the whole human race into Daleks, but I managed to make some of the Daleks think they were human. Result – Dalek civil war.

Family of Blood, the

Oh, this lot just wouldn't give up. I mean, I tried. I ran away from them and hid – what more could I do? From a short-lived race, they wanted to steal my longevity and that wasn't going to happen. They found me, even though I'd taken on the identity of a teacher called John Smith. Sent deadly Scarecrows after me and my friends. So I had to sort them out. Pity, but they didn't leave me any choice.

D E F

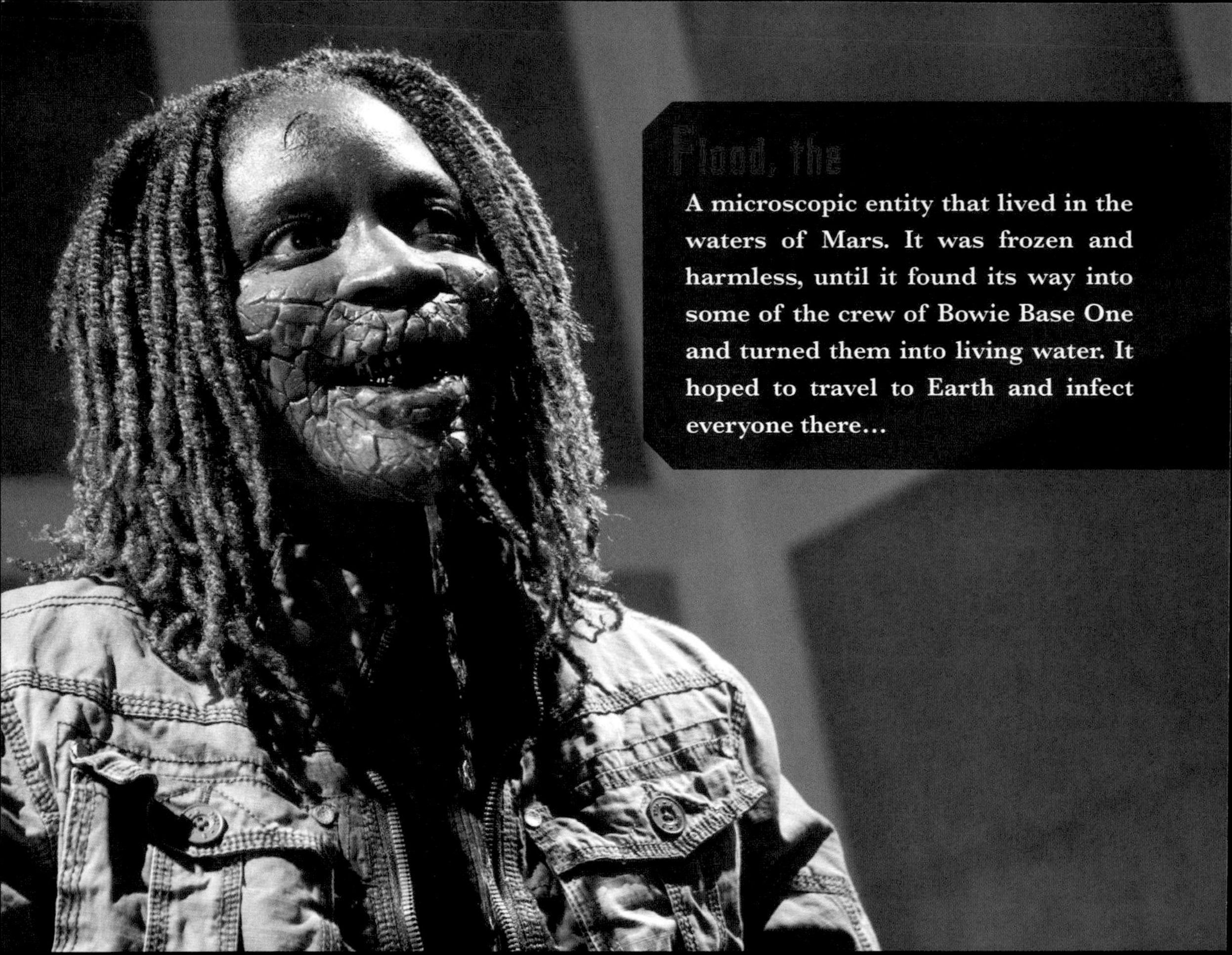

Flood, the

A microscopic entity that lived in the waters of Mars. It was frozen and harmless, until it found its way into some of the crew of Bowie Base One and turned them into living water. It hoped to travel to Earth and infect everyone there...

Gelth

An ethereal race that lost their bodies during the Time War. They could animate the bodies of the dead – zombies, ugh! They pretended to want a peaceful solution to their body problem, but actually they wanted to invade Earth. Typical.

Hartigan, Miss

She was the Matron of the St Joseph's Workhouse in Victorian London. But she was ambitious – oh, so ambitious. She had some good ideas about equality, mind – about how men shouldn't be so much more privileged than women. A bit ahead of her time, to be honest. But her solution was rather extreme – she teamed up with the Cybermen. That was never going to work. She wanted social change, they wanted to drain her of all emotion.

Headless Monks

Monks. With no heads. Which kind of figures. They're from the Delirium Archive, and they keep their heads in special boxes – no, really. They worked with Madame Kovarian and her lot to try to track me down – and kidnapped Amy, which wasn't on. Not on at all.

Jagrafess

Or to give him his full title, the Mighty Jagrafess of the Holy Hadrojassic Maxarodenfoe. A huge creature installed in the top of Satellite Five that controlled all the media and communications for Earth in the time of the Fourth 'Great and Beautiful' Earth Empire.

Kovarian, Madame

What a nasty lady. She worked with the Silence to kidnap Amy, and then take away her daughter, Melody Pond. Brainwashed her into becoming an assassin programmed to kill me. I mean, convoluted or what? But there again, I suppose it worked – River Song did end up killing me. Or so everyone thought…

Krafayis

Hunters and scavengers. The Krafayis are invisible to most people, though my friend Vincent van Gogh could see the injured Krafayis that was stranded in France. But then he had a unique way of looking at the world, didn't he?

Krillitanes

The Krillitanes are super-evolutionary. They restructure themselves, taking the best bits from the races they conquer. The last time I met them they were like large bats. With big teeth. Unfortunately for them, they've evolved to the point where the oil they secrete is actually poisonous to them – deadly. Blows them up. Bang!

K

Lumic, John

Scientist who invented the Cybermen on an alternate Earth. He wanted humans to take the next evolutionary step and become Human Point 2. Being in the communications industry, I suppose he thought the best way for that to happen was through a software and hardware upgrade. But the software was people's brains and the hardware was their bodies.

Macra

Huge – and I mean enormous humungous huge – creatures, a bit like crabs. Only bigger, obviously. And they feed on gas. Nasty toxic noxious gas. They were known as the scourge of Galaxy M87, though the last lot I came across was in New New York on New Earth. I think they'd escaped from the zoo. Probably. They were living in the exhaust fumes beneath the main motorway.

Master, the

Perhaps the only other Time Lord who survived the Great Time War. We were at school together, long, long ago. But we went off in very different ways after that. The Master stands for everything that I fight against. He's a troublemaker. He delights in chaos and carnage and craves nothing but power. Having said all that, he can be perfectly charming.

Ood, the

Telepathic inhabitants of the Ood-Sphere. They have two brains – imagine that. One of them they have to carry around. Very carefully. And that left them wide open to being exploited by the unscrupulous Ood Operations company, which turned them into slaves, apparently happy to serve humanity. Maybe they would have been happy to help – but you have to give them a choice.

Peg Dolls

George was a Tenza, though he didn't realise it. He thought he was a little boy. But he could use his Tenza powers to bring toys to life, or turn people into toys – like the Peg Dolls inside a dolls' house inside the cupboard in his bedroom.

Pig Slaves

When the Daleks of the Cult of Skaro escaped to New York in the 1930s, they created slaves to help them build a new race of Human-Daleks. Those humans who weren't suitable to become Human-Daleks they turned into slaves – Pig Slaves. No, really. They merged them with pigs to create creatures that were subservient but rather dim.

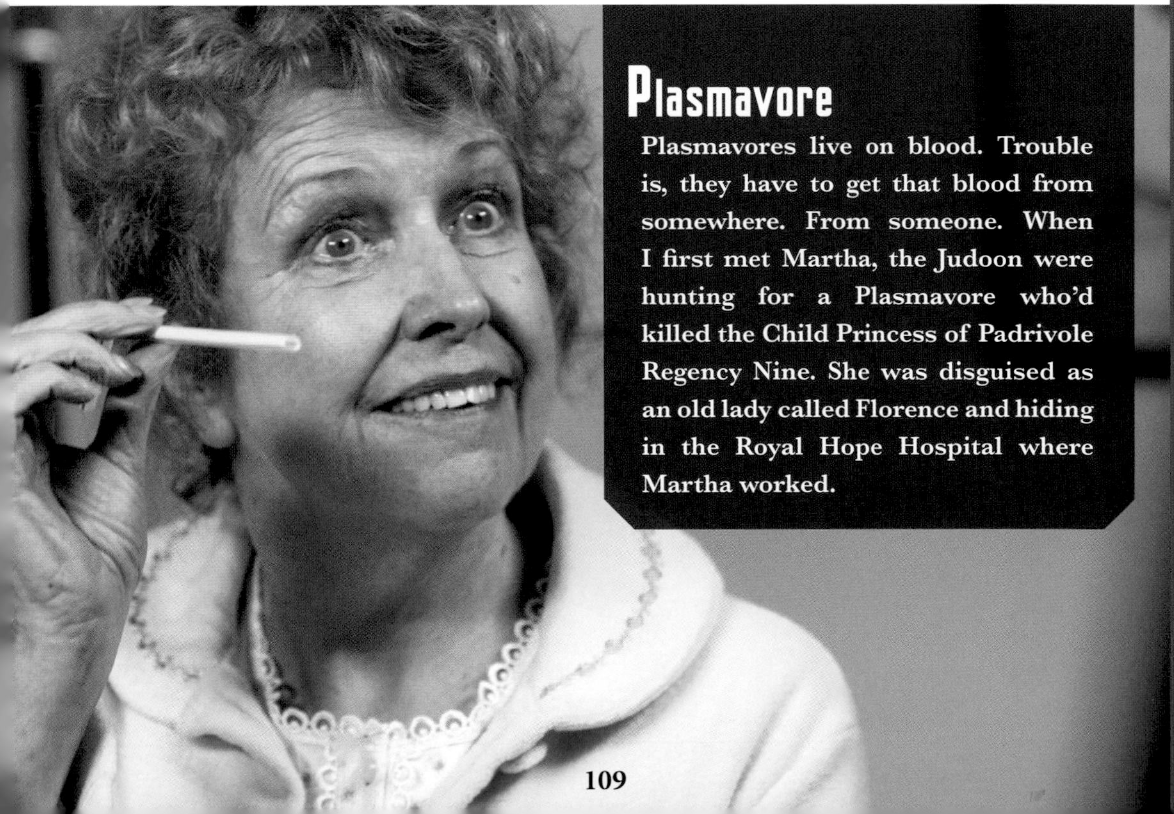

Plasmavore

Plasmavores live on blood. Trouble is, they have to get that blood from somewhere. From someone. When I first met Martha, the Judoon were hunting for a Plasmavore who'd killed the Child Princess of Padrivole Regency Nine. She was disguised as an old lady called Florence and hiding in the Royal Hope Hospital where Martha worked.

Prisoner Zero

A prisoner of the Atraxi. Not sure where the 'Zero' bit came from, but anyway... In its true form Prisoner Zero was a sort of jellified snake thing. But it was a multiform so it could change to look like a mother and her children, or a man and a dog – provided they were joined by holding hands or a lead or something. Only Prisoner Zero kept getting confused, so the man barked and the dog spoke. That sort of thing.

Pyroviles

Large creatures made of living, molten rock. They came from Pyrovilia, and when their world disappeared (taken by the Daleks), they looked for a new one. And they rather liked Earth. They established a base under Mount Vesuvius in Pompeii, Italy. Which maybe wasn't such a wise move as they were destroyed along with Pompeii when Mount Vesuvius erupted in 79AD.

Racnoss

Large, multi-legged creatures, a bit like spiders. Only much bigger and not really like spiders at all. For one thing they were around in the Dark Times – billions of years ago. Hungry things, they'd eat their way through a whole planet when they were born... That's probably why the Fledgling Empires went to war with the Racnoss and wiped them out. Or almost – the Empress survived, in hibernation aboard her Webstar.

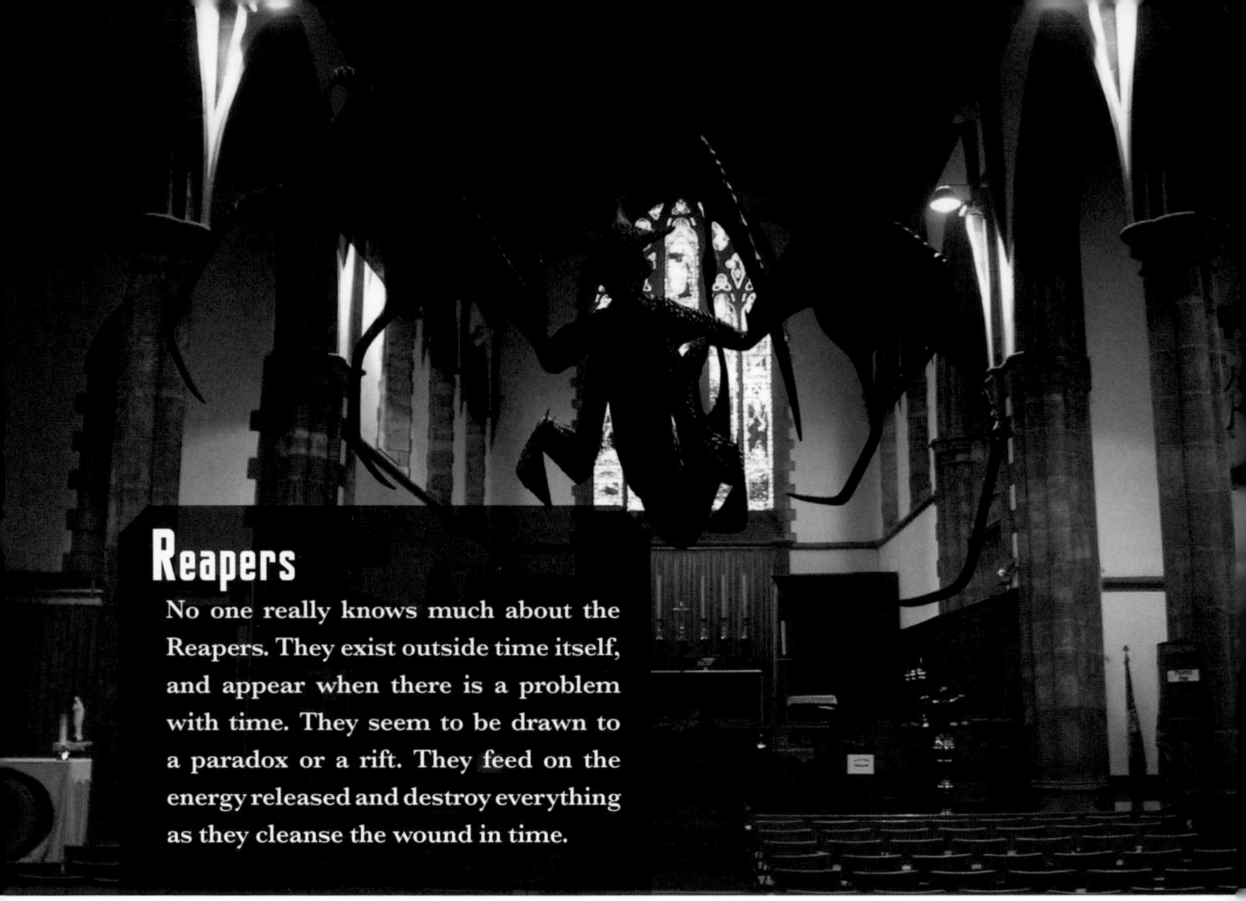

Reapers

No one really knows much about the Reapers. They exist outside time itself, and appear when there is a problem with time. They seem to be drawn to a paradox or a rift. They feed on the energy released and destroy everything as they cleanse the wound in time.

Santa Robot

OK, they only looked like Santa because of the way they dressed. And the beards – yes, I'll give you the beards. But really they were Pilot Fish robots, scavenging for the power they needed to keep them alive. The Empress of the Racnoss cottoned on to that when she arrived, and took them over, using them to help her hatch out the last of her race.

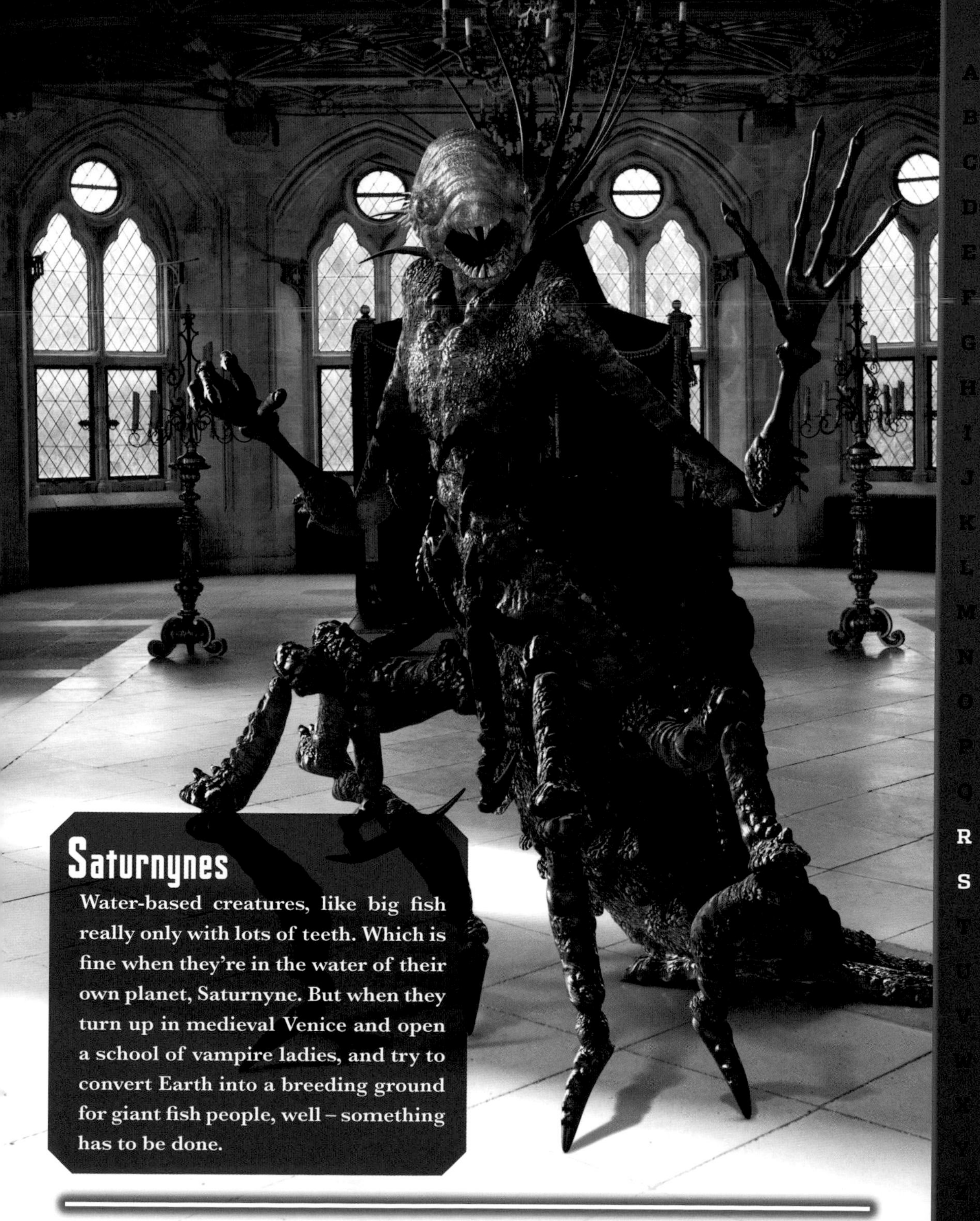

Saturnynes

Water-based creatures, like big fish really only with lots of teeth. Which is fine when they're in the water of their own planet, Saturnyne. But when they turn up in medieval Venice and open a school of vampire ladies, and try to convert Earth into a breeding ground for giant fish people, well – something has to be done.

Silence, the

What is it with the Silence? What have they got against me, I mean – what? They seem to go to an awful lot of trouble just to cause me grief. They must know I'll sort them out eventually. Unless they've forgotten. Then again, the thing about the Silence is that you forget them. As soon as you can't see them, you forget they were ever there. Makes it tricky trying to escape from them, and even harder to fight them.

Slitheen

A criminal family from the planet Raxacoricofallapatorius. Not a very pleasant lot. They were all sentenced to death in their absence, which gives you some idea. First time I met them, they had these skin suits so they could pretend to be important politicians and policemen and so on. They planned to use Earth's own nuclear weapons to destroy it, and then sell the remains on as rocket fuel. Unscrupulous bunch.

Siren

The Siren that captivated the sailors of Captain Avery's crew was really an alien medic. She – well, she chose to look like a 'she' – was from a spaceship in the same space as Avery's ship but in another dimension. If you follow. Or even if you don't actually. The crew thought she was killing them when they were wounded. But actually she was detecting the wound and taking them off for treatment. Ah, sweet.

Sontarans

A race of cloned warriors dedicated to warfare. They've been at war with their enemy, the Rutan Host, for so long that no one can remember what they're fighting over. But that doesn't stop them. Nasty, brutish and short – the only way to stun a Sontaran is with a blow to the probic vent on the back of the neck. Good luck with that.

S

Spiders

I've met so many spiders. Some nicer than others. Cassandra used metal spider robots to sabotage Platform One. Well, I call them Spiders but they only had four legs and one camera eye, so they weren't really spiders, I suppose. The Giant Spiders of Metebelis Three though – now those are spiders.

Stingrays

Flying scavengers, the stingray-like creatures that devastated San Helios and many other worlds will eat anything. Anything at all. They fly round the world, devouring everything they come across – and going so fast they open up a wormhole that will take them on to their next victim world.

Sycorax

More scavengers – there's a lot of them about. The Sycorax are an ancient race of warriors that travel through space in their rock-like spacecraft and enslave the races they come across. They don't mind a good fight, but they prefer to conquer planets without conflict – tricking world leaders into accepting Sycorax terms. Sneaky.

Toclafane

The Toclafane was a name the Master gave to what the human race will become in billions of years' time. The shrivelled remains of a human, housed inside a spherical flying life-support system. The Master created a temporal paradox so that he could bring the Toclafane back through time to enslave their own ancestors. Only the Master could think up a diabolical plan like that!

Vashta Nerada

The piranhas of the air. Creatures that hide in, and create, shadows. They are a swarm of darkness itself, that can strip a body bare of flesh in an instant. Then they can animate the remaining fleshless husk. The creatures' spores hatch inside living wood, becoming a swarm in minutes. But they can survive in the wood even after the trees are cut down – so they can live in paper made from that wood. Be careful next time you open a book...

Weeping Angels

Also known as the Lonely Assassins. The Weeping Angels are quantum locked. It's a defence mechanism. They only move when you're not watching them. When you can see them, they turn to stone – so they look and feel and act just like statues. But turn away, look in another direction, and they will come after you. In a flash. In the blink of an eye. So, whatever you do –

DON'T BLINK

Werewolf

The Werewolf that Rose and I saved Queen Victoria from was actually a life form from another world. It fell to Earth in 1540, and was worshipped by the local monks of the Glen of St Catherine. It took a human host, and drawing on local legends, it mapped itself on to a creature that became a ravening wolf whenever there was a full moon…

Wire, the

An alien criminal, denied a body by its fellow kind, that came to Earth in a bolt of lightning. The Wire fed on electricity – even the electrical activity of the brain. It stole people's faces – no, really. Poor Rose lost her face for a while. The Wire planned to use the television coverage of the 1953 coronation of Queen Elizabeth II to reach out from TV sets and steal the electrical activity from millions of brains to give it the life essence it needed. Lucky I was there, eh?!

People – and Aliens and Whatever – who are Sort of Nice Sometimes. You know?

Not so sure about these. Well, you probably got that from the section title, didn't you? So, you could be OK, but watch your step – those of you who have feet.

Adipose

Ah, sweet. But not when you know where they came from. Be careful of miracle diet plans, that's all I'm saying, OK? If it sounds too good to be true then it's probably, well, too good to be true. Like the Adipose Diet. It actually created little Adipose children out of your spare fat. Only it didn't stop there… Nasty.

Cassandra

Lady Cassandra O'Brien Dot Delta Seventeen was the last pure-born human, or so she claimed. Not that she looked very human when Rose and I first met her. She'd had so many cosmetic operations that all that was left of her was a piece of skin stretched across a frame with her brain in a tank underneath.

Cat People

You find a lot of these on New Earth. The Sisters of Plenitude who run the hospital there, for example – they're all cats. Big cats. Dressed as nuns. It's all a bit disconcerting, actually.

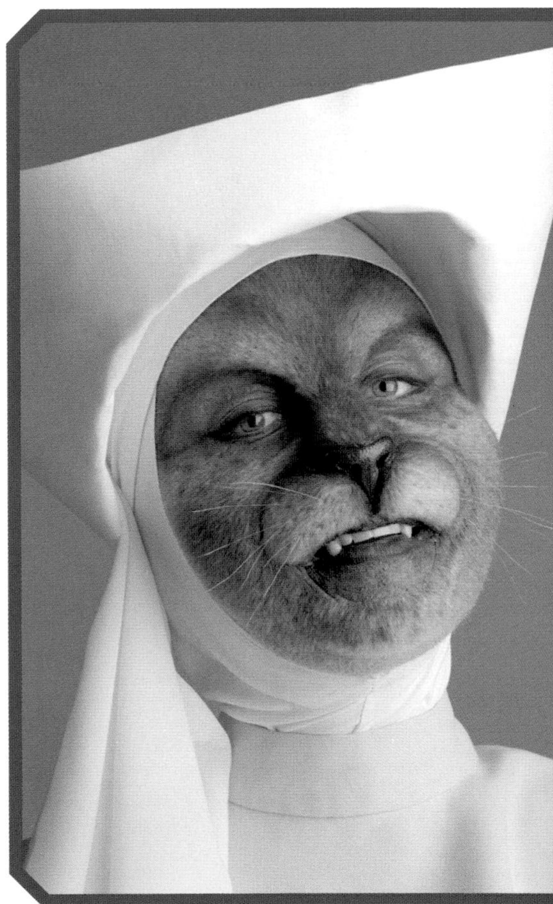

Ganger

Short for doppelgänger, which means 'double' in German. Gangers were the copies of people made from the Flesh. The whole process didn't work quite like it said in the instructions. I should know – I've had a Ganger of my own, you know. Very strange experience.

Hartman, Yvonne

In charge of the Torchwood Institute, or at least the London branch, when the Cybermen invaded from another universe. Closely followed by the Daleks. So she rather had her work cut out for her – especially as she was more concerned with hunting me down at the time. She ended up as a Cyberman, but that didn't stop her doing her duty as she saw it. Single-minded, or what?!

Hath

They're fish. Maybe not actual fish, but aquatic certainly. When they leave the water – like to go and colonise other worlds working with the expanding Human Empire – then they have to wear special masks and breathe oxygenated liquid. Makes it quite tricky to communicate with them as everything sounds sort of bubbly.

Heavenly Host

Robots that look like angels, how cool is that? With a halo and wings and everything. The Heavenly Host – or just the Host for short – were the information points and general automated helpers on board Max Capricorn cruise-liner spaceships. Which is fine and dandy unless they get reprogrammed to attack the crew and passengers, like on the *Titanic*. Then it all gets a bit unpleasant.

Humans

You probably know more about humans than I do. What an inventive, invincible species. Nothing stops you lot. Oh, the things you'll achieve, the empires you'll have. Yes, there will be – and has been – injustice and bloodshed. But despite all that there's an admirable determination and ambition. You're indomitable.

Judoon

Rhino Space Police. That's pretty much it. They provide security for the Shadow Proclamation and hire themselves out to galactic governments to track down criminals and bring them to justice. They're enthusiastic in their approach, I'd say. In a shoot-first-and-ask-questions-afterwards sort of way. Where the Judoon are concerned, justice is always swift.

Lazarus, Professor

He meant well, did Professor Lazarus. He just wanted to change what it meant to be human. But that's a little bit ambitious and a big bit dangerous. He tinkered with his own genetic make-up, which is never a good move. Yes, he changed into a younger man. But a younger man who then turned into a huge homicidal monster. Not recommended.

Scarecrow

Not usually something to be scared of. Unless you're a crow, of course. The Master once disguised himself as a scarecrow, you know. I never did work out why. But he's like that – he'd burn down your kitchen to boil an egg... Then there was the army of scarecrows the Family of Blood brought to life and sent after me. Molecular Fringe Animation – a powerful but unpleasant technique. But then they were a powerful but unpleasant family...

Silurians / Earth Reptiles Homo Reptilia / Sea Devils

What do we call them? It seems to vary every time we meet. But the Silurians (or Earth Reptiles, or Homo Reptilia or if they're the underwater sort then maybe Sea Devils) were the original intelligent inhabitants of Earth. You humans evolved while they were all in hibernation and when some of them occasionally wake up they discover their planet has been overrun by upstart apes.
No offence.

A B C D E F G H I J K L M N O P Q R S T U V W X Y Z

Smilers

Information points on *Starship UK*. They look like wooden figures sitting inside glass booths. Smiling – hence 'Smiler'. Except sometimes they get a bit nasty. Then the head rotates to show a face that isn't smiling. More of a hostile grimace. And if that wasn't worrying enough, they can stand up and come out of their booths to get you...

Vespiform

An ancient and wise race from the Silfrax Galaxy. The Vespiform are amorphic. They can look just like you or me – well, maybe not me because that obviously takes huge skill and getting the hair right could be a problem. But when they're being themselves, as it were, they're like giant wasps. And I mean huge-giant wasps. With a nasty sting in the tail. A rolled up newspaper just won't do the job with a Vespiform.

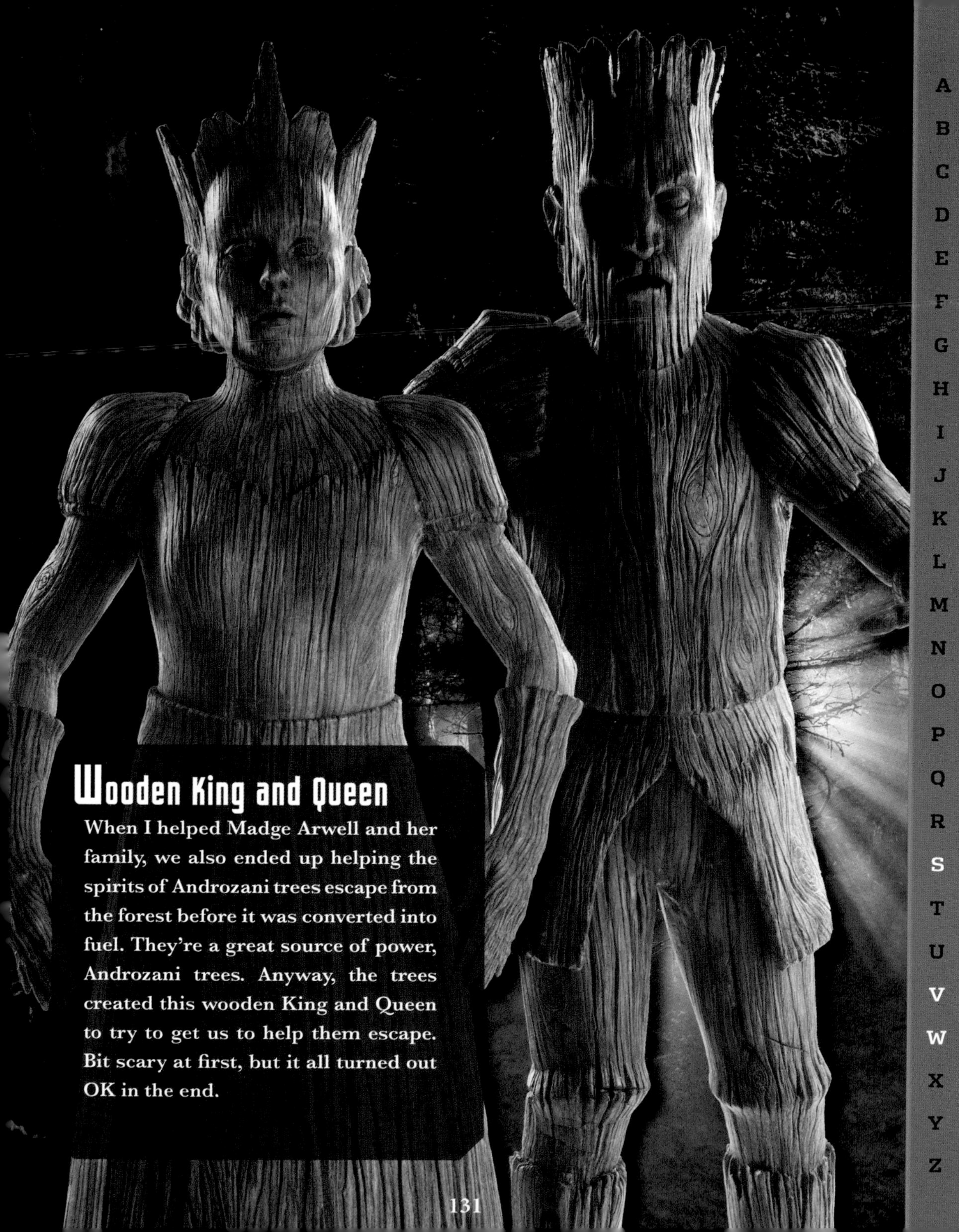

Wooden King and Queen

When I helped Madge Arwell and her family, we also ended up helping the spirits of Androzani trees escape from the forest before it was converted into fuel. They're a great source of power, Androzani trees. Anyway, the trees created this wooden King and Queen to try to get us to help them escape. Bit scary at first, but it all turned out OK in the end.

Organisations and Groups

Well, what it says really. Here's just a few organisations and groups that you might need to know about – either because they can help, or because you should avoid them at all costs. You'll have to work out which is which for yourself as I'm not doing colour-coding or anything clever like that.

Blue Peter

OK, so not really a group as such. But one of the greatest television programmes ever in the history of television. It's just fantastic – they show you how to make things with sticky tape and old washing-up liquid bottles and all sorts. They even made a Slitheen spaceship once – brilliant!

CIA

The Central Intelligence Agency in the United States of America. Bunch of spies. Not to be confused with the FBI. Or with the other CIA.

CIA (er, other one)

The other CIA – the real CIA as far as I'm concerned – is the Time Lords' Celestial Intervention Agency. It's completely different from the human USA version. On Gallifrey, the CIA was a bunch of time spies.

Cybus Industries

Technology and communications company run by John Lumic on an alternate version of Earth. The company was responsible for creating and building the Cybermen in that universe – and they're named after the company.

CUBUS INDUSTRIES

FBI

The US Federal Bureau of Investigation. Like the CIA, but it operates within the USA whereas the CIA works outside the USA. Bunch of agents.

LINDA

The London Investigation 'N' Detective Agency. I know, I know – the letters don't quite work properly, do they? Tell that to Elton Pope who thought of it. It was set up to investigate me, actually. I guess that sort of worked – apart from the Abzorbaloff getting involved and absorbing most of the members of the team, that is.

Ood Operations

Company based on the Ood-Sphere and run by its chairman, Klineman Halpen. It took 'natural' Ood and removed their hind-brains so that they became docile and servile. The company then sold them on as slaves. Not a great way to run a business, and I sorted it out as soon as I could – with more than a little help from the Ood themselves.

A B C D E F G H I J K L M N O P Q R S T U V W X Y Z

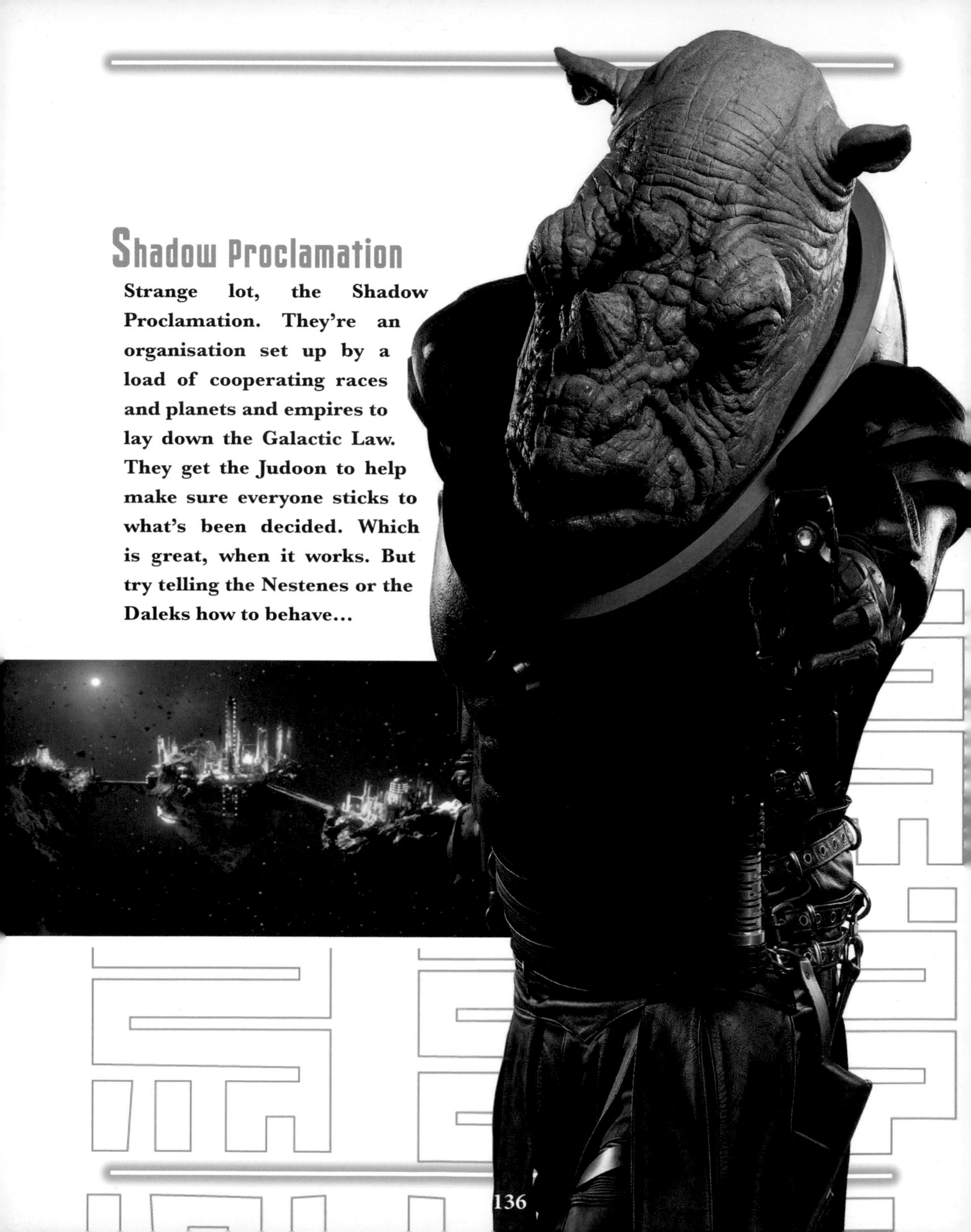

Shadow Proclamation

Strange lot, the Shadow Proclamation. They're an organisation set up by a load of cooperating races and planets and empires to lay down the Galactic Law. They get the Judoon to help make sure everyone sticks to what's been decided. Which is great, when it works. But try telling the Nestenes or the Daleks how to behave...

Silver Cloak, the

Good old Wilf. He got all his elderly friends who had a bit of time on their hands to keep an eye out for me. Called it 'The Silver Cloak', though I'm not sure why. Lovely bunch of people. Though that Minnie Hooper is a bit… enthusiastic.

Sisters of Plenitude, the

We did Cat People, didn't we? Right, well, I probably said then – Sisters of Plenitude: Cat Nuns who run a hospital on New Earth. In New New York, in fact. Though I did have to take issue with some of the treatments, or at least the way they developed them. Hardly ethical.

Sybilline Sisterhood

Another group of ladies, this time in Pompeii, Italy, in Roman times. Worshipped the Sybilline Oracle, but their high priestess got contaminated by the Pyroviles hiding under Mount Vesuvius. On the plus side that meant she really could see into the future. But there's always a downside – in this case she was turned to living stone.

Time Agency, the

Shadowy lot, the Time Agency. I have to confess I don't know a lot about them. Except that Captain Jack Harkness used to work for them, until they wiped his memory and chucked him out. They use Vortex Manipulators, which are just so not-cool compared with a TARDIS.

Torchwood Institute

Set up by Queen Victoria to defend the British Empire from alien threats and menaces. They were also on the lookout for me, as Queen Vic wasn't so happy I got her involved with that werewolf thing. Captain Jack works for Torchwood, so they're not all bad.

TORCHWOOD

INSTITUTE

UNIT

A bit like Torchwood, but more official and international. The Unified Intelligence Taskforce is a military operation run from Geneva, Switzerland. The British contingent used to be commanded by my old friend Brigadier Lethbridge-Stewart. I even worked for them for a while, as Scientific Advisor. Unpaid, of course.

Spacestations and Space Bases and So On

If you're travelling the universe, you might end up on or in one of these, so it's best to know about them. Again, it's just a sample. And I'm not convinced this alphabetical order thing really helps much. But there again, you can take comfort from the fact that in Ancient High Gallifreyan they're all in a completely different order anyway.

Bowie Base One

Set up on Mars in 2058 under the command of Captain Adelaide Brooke, Bowie Base One was named after singer David Bowie – who had a song called 'Life on Mars' which did very well. Which is ironic really, because it was the life on Mars, in the form of the Flood, that killed off most of the crew.

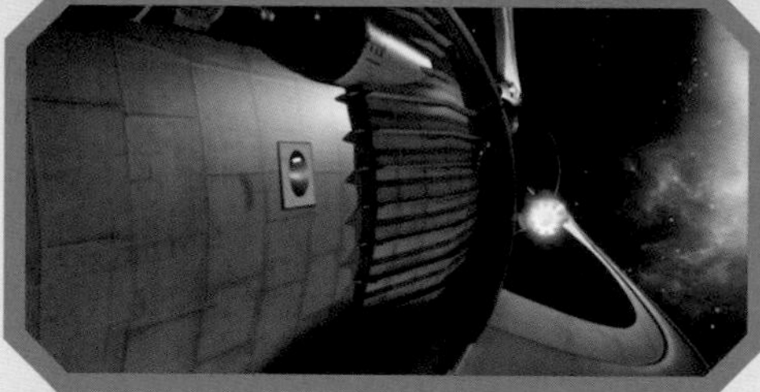

Byzantium, the

I rescued River Song from the *Byzantium*. Well, I had the TARDIS there ready where she was blasted out of it into space. She'd left me a message on its Home Box (look it up – it's in here somewhere). The ship then crashed. But that didn't destroy the Weeping Angel that was on-board.

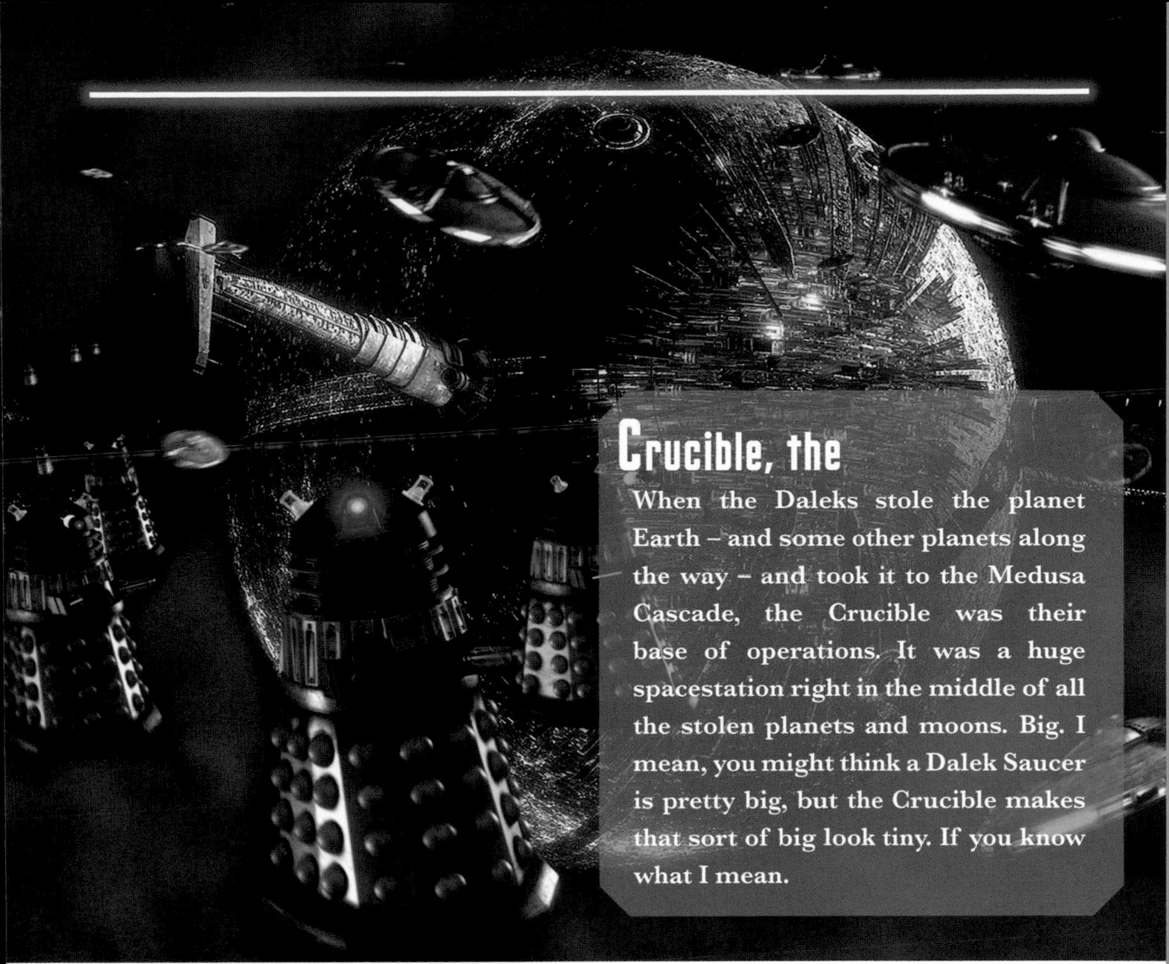

Crucible, the

When the Daleks stole the planet Earth – and some other planets along the way – and took it to the Medusa Cascade, the Crucible was their base of operations. It was a huge spacestation right in the middle of all the stolen planets and moons. Big. I mean, you might think a Dalek Saucer is pretty big, but the Crucible makes that sort of big look tiny. If you know what I mean.

Platform One

There were fifteen 'Platform's. I think. Anyway, however many there were, Platform One was the first. Hence 'Platform One'. See? Big spacestation that served as a hotel, conference centre, meeting place blah blah blah. I watched the end of the world from it. Earth burned away by the sun. Or I would have done, if I hadn't been busy with more important things like staying alive and saving Rose and everyone else on-board.

Sanctuary Base 6

The Sanctuary Bases were all built from prefabricated components. So one looks pretty much identical to another. But the interesting thing about Sanctuary Base 6 was that it was on this impossible planet that used to be called Krop Tor orbiting a black hole. Orbiting a black hole – not falling into it, like it should have done. There was a clue there that everything wasn't quite right. Which it certainly wasn't.

Satellite Five / The Game Station

It was the same place, you see. Just a hundred years apart. Satellite Five broadcast all sorts of news to the human empire. But by the time it had been renamed the Game Station it was all rather downmarket – panel shows and quiz games. Mostly unpleasant ones in which people got hurt or even died. Not nice at all. So I shouldn't have been too surprised that the Daleks were behind it all.

Starship UK

When you humans evacuated the Earth – or at least, one of the times you evacuated the Earth – you all left on spaceships from each of the main countries. *Starship UK*, for whatever reason, had a few problems and wasn't actually completely finished in time. But luckily a bit of help turned up in the form of a Star Whale. So the UK population all escaped by whale power. Except Scotland – they wanted their own spaceship.

Have You Visited...?

In your free time, while travelling through time and space – if that's what you're up to – then here are a few places you might want to check out. They're not all as tranquil and beautiful as the Eye of Orion, I'm afraid. Which is why I'm keeping that one for myself and haven't even put it on the list – so shhhhh, don't tell anyone!

Apalapucia

Ah, what a planet. Hub of ten thousand cultures and a great holiday destination. Things to do, places to go, people to see. That is, until the Chen 7 virus blighted the place. Well, how was I to know? I didn't expect Amy to get separated from us into a different time stream that was running faster. I didn't know she'd be stuck there for decades, chased by deadly Handbots (even though they were only trying to help).

Barcelona

No, not the one in Spain. This Barcelona is a planet. It's great – the dogs have no noses. How do they smell? Er, let's not go there – everyone, and I mean everyone, does that joke. All the time. It does get a bit wearing after a while, I'll admit.

Cardiff

I've been to Cardiff a few times. Sometimes on purpose, because there's a useful time rift left over from that business with... Well, let's just say there's a useful time rift so I can park the TARDIS over it and fuel her up when I need to. Captain Jack's Torchwood mob were based there too for a while. Oh, and it was the first place I took Rose back in time to see. That wasn't quite so deliberate, but she did get to meet Charles Dickens.

Chess Pits of Vegas 12, the

They play Live Chess. And 'live' means 'live'. The pieces are electrified. Take too long, or get into trouble, or... Well, you get the idea. I played a good game against Gantok there. I could have won, but I had to resign the game in the end so he'd take me to find Dorium Maldovar.

Delirium Archive, the

The final resting place of the Headless Monks. They turned it into a museum afterwards. A very good museum actually. Took Amy there once, but we had to cut our visit a bit short. There was some trouble with River Song, hallucinogenic lipstick, a crashing spaceship and a Weeping Angel. Usual sort of thing.

Demon's Run

Didn't enjoy my visit, if I'm perfectly honest. Demon's Run is an asteroid owned by the Headless Monks. It's where Madame Kovarian and the Silence took Amy when they kidnapped her and replaced her with a copy made from the Flesh. If you remember that. If you don't – keep up!

Earth

My favourite planet. No, really. It took me a long time to realise that was why I kept coming back – or why the TARDIS kept bringing me back. But yes, there's nowhere else quite like Earth. Even New Earth isn't really like Earth Earth. You are so so lucky to live there. OK, some places on Earth are better than others, but hey.

Fields of Trenzalore, the

I've never been, and I'm sort of avoiding it to be honest. There's all that talk and rumours and legends of the Fall of the Eleventh and all that. Not that I'm paranoid, not that I'm running away or anything. So one day maybe. But not yet.

Gallifrey

The Shining World of the Seven Systems. Home of the Time Lords – until it was destroyed in the last Great Time War. I know I took a TARDIS and ran away, but it was home. Such a beautiful place, with its two suns, orange sky, red grass, silver-leafed trees and snow-topped mountains… Maybe I wasn't there very often, but I do miss it.

House

I don't really know what House was. It wasn't a place, it was a sentience, a life form, a series of thoughts. But it possessed an asteroid in a bubble universe. It drew the TARDIS there – tricked me into going, in fact. But it was the TARDIS that House was after. Got more than it bargained for, I have to say.

Krop Tor

The so-called Impossible Planet because it orbited a black hole. I told you about it, remember? Or don't you read these things in order? Maybe you don't, maybe you just dip in or look up stuff in an emergency. Well, good luck with that. So go and look up the Beast. Krop Tor – impossible planet – black hole – Santuary Base 6 – Beast. OK?

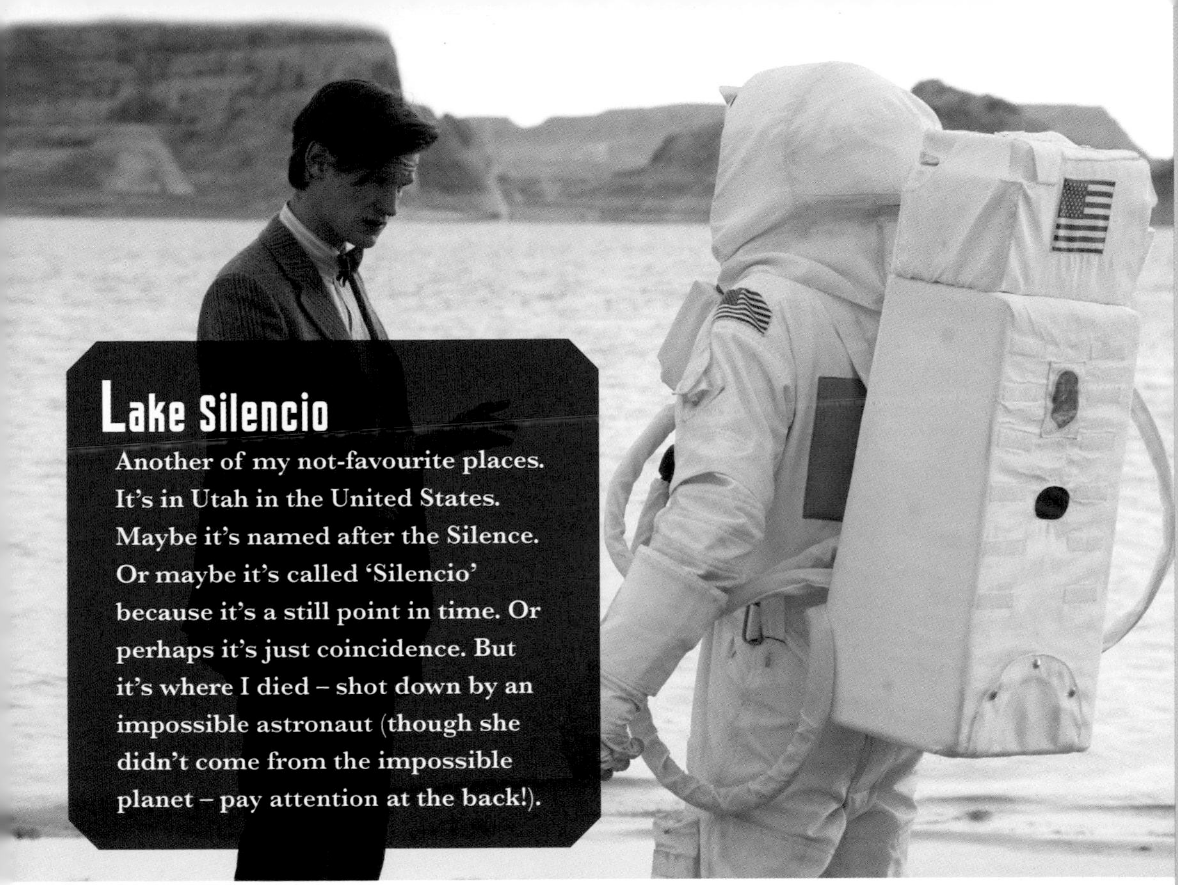

Lake Silencio

Another of my not-favourite places. It's in Utah in the United States. Maybe it's named after the Silence. Or maybe it's called 'Silencio' because it's a still point in time. Or perhaps it's just coincidence. But it's where I died – shot down by an impossible astronaut (though she didn't come from the impossible planet – pay attention at the back!).

Leadworth

Lovely little village in Gloucestershire. It's got a village green, and a duck pond, an old people's home, and even a little hospital. Charming place. Quaint – that's the word for it. Quaint. Oh, and it's where Amy and Rory grew up and lived. River too, actually, but that gets a bit more tricky because she wasn't River then, she was Melody and Amy named River after Melody who was actually River all along. I think I'll stop now before it gets too complicated.

A B C D E F G H I J K L M N O P Q R S T U V W X Y Z

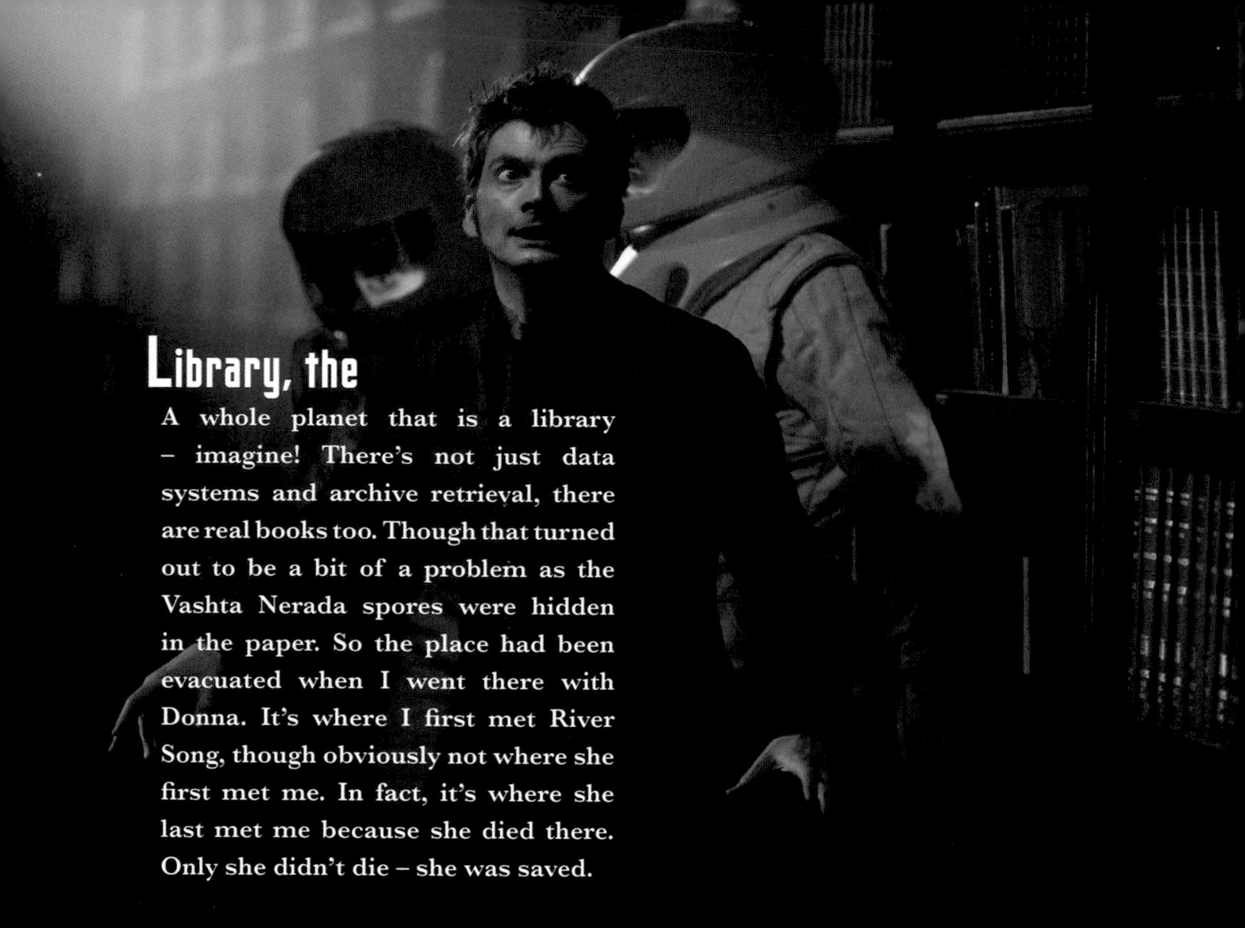

Library, the

A whole planet that is a library – imagine! There's not just data systems and archive retrieval, there are real books too. Though that turned out to be a bit of a problem as the Vashta Nerada spores were hidden in the paper. So the place had been evacuated when I went there with Donna. It's where I first met River Song, though obviously not where she first met me. In fact, it's where she last met me because she died there. Only she didn't die – she was saved.

Medusa Cascade, the

Spectacular. A rift point in space. I went there as a child when I was about ninety. Loved it. Always meant to go back – promised to take Donna, for one. When I did go back though it didn't really live up to expectations. But that was because the Daleks had parked twenty-seven stolen planets there and were planning to blow up the whole of reality. That sort of thing rather spoils the view.

Messaline

Full scale war when I went there. Humans and Hath had fought each other for generations (though that wasn't actually very long, as it turned out). But they should have it all sorted and terraformed and lovely by now.

Midnight

Beautiful but deadly. It's like a giant diamond hanging in space. The Pleasure Palace is very comfy with all mod cons. But you can't go outside or you'll die from the X-tonic Radiation. Worth taking a Crusader Tour though to see the sights in perfect safety. Well, usually.

New Earth

In Galaxy M87, and not a patch on the original, of course. Though it's about the same size. But there's a lot to recommend it – like the apple grass. Where else in the universe do you get apple grass? Oh, the smell's lovely. The smell of the motorway, on the other hand – not so lovely.

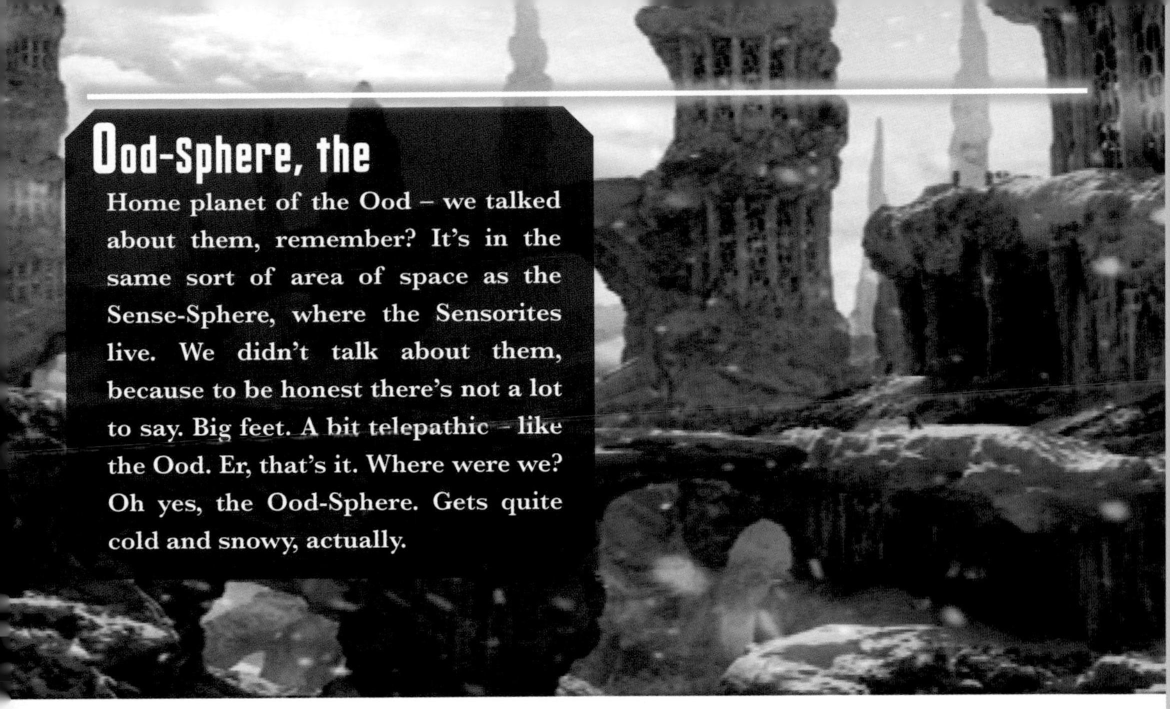

Ood-Sphere, the

Home planet of the Ood – we talked about them, remember? It's in the same sort of area of space as the Sense-Sphere, where the Sensorites live. We didn't talk about them, because to be honest there's not a lot to say. Big feet. A bit telepathic – like the Ood. Er, that's it. Where were we? Oh yes, the Ood-Sphere. Gets quite cold and snowy, actually.

Pompeii

A town in the Compania region of Italy. On Earth. Not far from where Naples is today. Pompeii is famous really because it isn't there any more. Not as a town where people live and work and play and eat and tell jokes. It was destroyed by the eruption of Mount Vesuvius in AD79. I was there – it was a terrible shame, but there was no other way to stop the Pyroviles taking over the whole of the planet. Even so, not my finest hour. So, Pompeii – lovely place to visit. But avoid Volcano Day.

Raxacoricofallapatorius

Home, not surprisingly I suppose, of Raxacoricofallapatorians. Did I spell that right? Yes, I think so. You've probably heard of the Slitheen, maybe of the Blathereen and other Raxacoricofallapatorian families. Families are big there. I don't mean they have big families – though they do – but they're important. Quite right too.

San Helios

Beautiful planet in the Scorpion Nebula. Three suns, so it gets hot. Thriving place. Very lush. San Helios city might not be very imaginatively named, but it's a lovely place. Or rather, it was. The whole planet got eaten by giant flying stingrays. Bit upset about that actually.

Sardicktown

The capital city of the Earth colony planet Ember. Named after Elliot Sardick. Funny family, the Sardicks. Though Elliot's son Kazran Sardick wasn't entirely beyond redemption, as it turned out...

Shan Shen

They have a great street market on Shan Shen. So much to see. Lots of great food. Hundreds of stalls. You have to be a bit careful though – 'buyer beware', that sort of thing. Donna went to get her fortune told, and ended up stuck in an alternate reality created by an alien Time Beetle from the Pantheon of Discord.

Skaro

Avoid. No, really – just don't go there. Well, it's absolutely crawling with Daleks for one thing. Their city stretches right across the desert, and underneath it too. But apart from that there's the Petrified Jungle, which isn't a whole lot of fun, some impressive but exhausting mountains, and the Lake of Mutations. Which is full of mutations. Not nice ones, either. Not like the Thals – though there are fewer and fewer of them these days. Sorry, rambling, now – just don't go there, OK?

Totters Lane

Not the most salubrious part of London, but it has a certain something. I used to live there – oh yes, at 76 Totters Lane. Actually, I'm not sure it really had a number. There was nothing at the end of the Lane, and that nothing was number 76. It was a junkyard, so a great place to leave the TARDIS where it wouldn't attract attention. No – no quips about the TARDIS and junk, please. Uncalled for, so stop it right now.

A B C D E F G H I J K L M N O P Q R S T U V W X Y Z

Hats and Other Cool Accessories

Cool is the new hot, and these are some of the hottest fashion accessories around. OK, so they might be out of fashion on Earth in your time, but somewhere, somewhen these are hot hot hot – which of course means that they are cool cool cool.

Astrakhan

Oh, a good warm hat. Though as it's made from the skin of karakul sheep, not as cool in the fashion sense as it used to be. I wore one, a long time ago. But then again, so did quite a lot of Soviet Politburo members. Warm, but worrying.

Bow tie

Now a bow tie really is cool. No matter what it's made from – well, within reason, obviously. If you don't have a bow tie, then get one immediately. Go on – now. Yes, girls too.

Fez

Short cylindrical hat made of red felt. With a tassel. A fez is cool too. Very popular in the Ottoman Empire, but it actually came from Greece originally. Did you know that? No, not many people do. But I do. I was there.

Floppy wide-brimmed hat

How versatile and useful is a floppy wide-brimmed hat? It'll keep the rain off, keep you warm, make you look cool while you're warm, and you can roll it up and put it in your pocket when you're not using it.

Recorder

No, not for recording things. Not one of those sorts of recorders. I mean a recorder – a musical instrument like a pipe with holes in. You blow down it and cover or uncover the holes to make different notes come out. There's a hole underneath it too which you have to keep covered. Which is a bit strange really – why put a hole there at all if you have to keep it covered? Why not just have no hole in the first place?

Scarf

A scarf will keep you warm too. Long thing, often made of wool, goes round your neck (but don't mess with things round your neck – you hear me?). I've had several scarves. My favourite, my absolute favourite was knitted for me by a witty little knitter called Madame Nostradamus. She said her husband could tell how much I was going to like it…

Shoes

Useful things, shoes. You can put your feet in them for one thing. Well, two things if you have two feet. They also make a great place to hide your TARDIS key when you're in hospital.

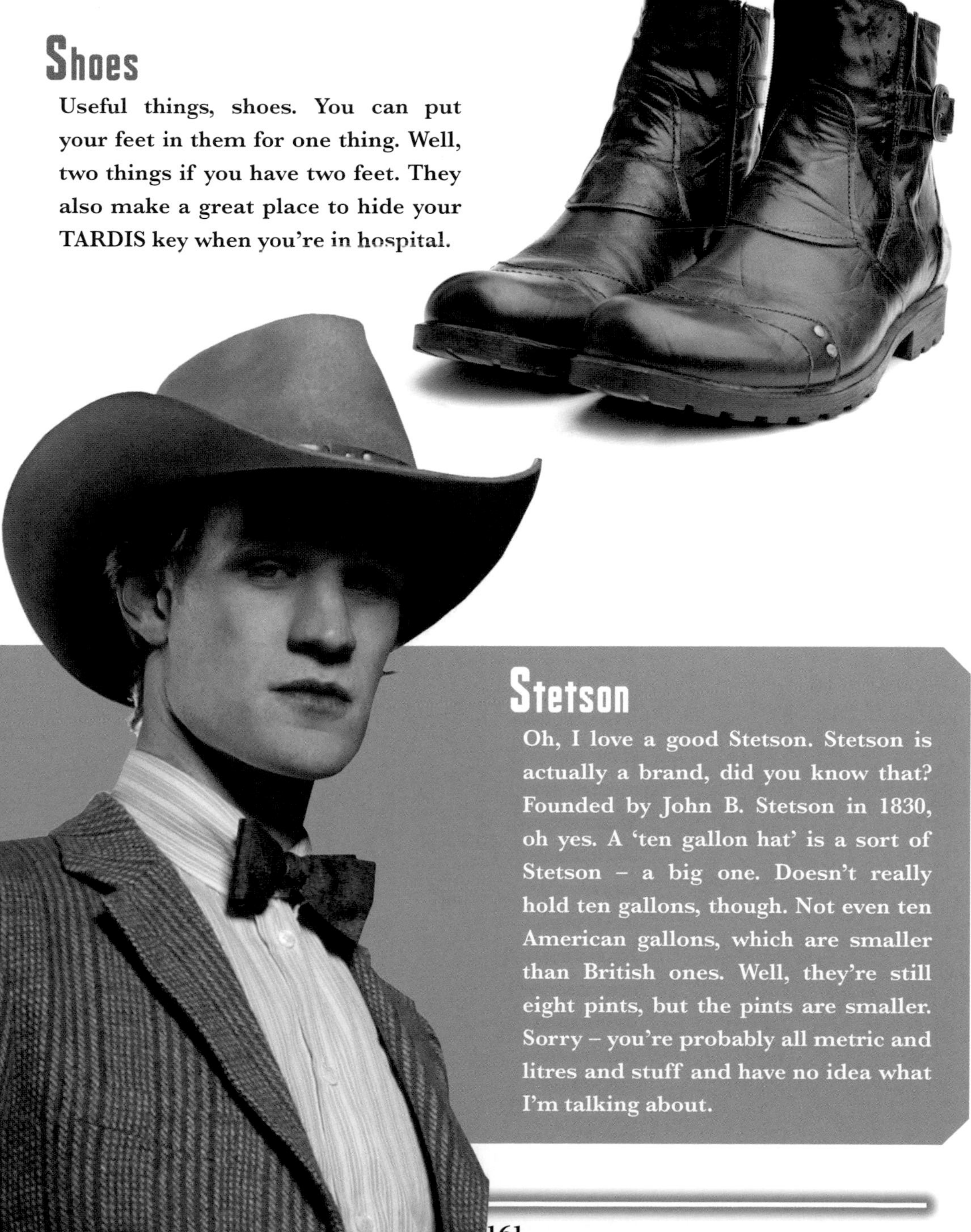

Stetson

Oh, I love a good Stetson. Stetson is actually a brand, did you know that? Founded by John B. Stetson in 1830, oh yes. A 'ten gallon hat' is a sort of Stetson – a big one. Doesn't really hold ten gallons, though. Not even ten American gallons, which are smaller than British ones. Well, they're still eight pints, but the pints are smaller. Sorry – you're probably all metric and litres and stuff and have no idea what I'm talking about.

Miscellaneous Humany-Wumany Type Stuff

As you're human (er – aren't you?) you probably understand these things better than I do. But just in case any of them have slipped through the cracks in your education, here you go...

200, the

You humans just love to refer to things by numbers, don't you? You do it all the time – 24/7. The 200 was actually a bus. Well, 200 is the route it was on in fact. Anyway, this bus – this particular 200 bus – got caught up in a wormhole thing and ended up stuck in the deserts of San Helios. Which certainly wasn't on the 200 route.

Biscuits

I love biscuits. All sorts of biscuits. Biscuit – it's from the French for 'twice cooked'. I don't cook biscuits myself so I have no idea why. The Americans call them 'cookies' so maybe they only cook them once. Unless cookie is short for 'twice-cookied' or something. Jammie Dodgers – they're the best.

Books

Books are so useful. I mean, what are you looking at now? Exactly. There will always be books. Maybe they won't always be made of paper, maybe eventually all the books will actually be data files of fast-access storage or whatever. But it's what is in the books that matters, isn't it? Reading – you have to do reading. If you don't read it's such a waste. If you don't read, then that's no better than not being able to read.

Christmas

What a great time, Christmas. Lots of planets have Christmas, even if they don't realise that's really what it is. All dates back to Winter drawing to an end and the daylight returning and the great feeling that gives you. Throw in a bit of religion too, and it's a magical time. Presents, good food, trees – when they're not trying to kill you… Father Christmas – when he's not trying to kill you. Actually, Christmas can get a bit hairy I've found. And I'm not talking about Santa's beard.

Edible Ball Bearings

What genius invented edible ball bearings? You get them on little cakes sometimes, don't you? Did you used to think you'd better pick them off or they'd break your teeth? Well, actually maybe they will. But – edible ball bearings. Woo-hoo!

Fish Finger Custard

If you've never dunked fish fingers in custard, you haven't lived. Do it now – no, seriously, go and do it now. Cook the fish fingers first, obviously. They're not good frozen. The custard can be hot or cold, doesn't matter. Both work. It doesn't just taste good, it's colour-coordinated too.

Football

Or 'footie' as my friend Craig sometimes calls it. I've played 'footie' with Craig and it was a lot of fun. I'm not sure I understand all the rules and everything yet – what's that offside thing all about, eh? But you get to kick a ball about and be in a team and get some fresh air and exercise in the park. I just hope it doesn't catch on so much it gets all commercial, because that would ruin the fun.

History

Now, 'history' to you is what's already happened. It's in the past, dead and gone. Interesting to read about and study, and probably very important in that it has shaped who and what you are. But once it's happened, that's it. As they say, it's, er, history. Things are a bit different for me though. History may not have happened yet, or not in the way you think it has. And things that are in your future might be history to me, and to other future people. If you're not careful it all gets a bit muddly-wuddly.

Laurel and Hardy

Weren't they great? Weren't they funny? They made old black and white films. Well, they weren't old films when they made them. And they made them in colour, only the camera could only do black and white. Now some people have gone back and coloured some of those old films in, which seems a bit pointless to me, because the people in them were never black and white. I should know – I was one of them. Appeared in *The Flying Deuces* back in 1939. Well, some prints of it, anyway. Or maybe that hasn't happened yet? (See 'History' opposite.)

Lodger

I've been a lodger. I have! It's when you go and live with someone else, like in their house or flat with your own room but maybe share a kitchen and telly and stuff. Obviously it's best to lodge with someone you get on with, or if it's your house or flat to have a lodger you get on with. Fortunately me and Craig got on like a house on fire. Well, not actually on fire – setting fire to your lodger or landlord's house isn't a great way to make sure you get on.

Love

Tricky one, love. But you'll know it when it happens. Because it's silly and wonderful, amazing and painful, difficult and easy, the most fantastically brilliantly heart-breaking thing ever.

Money

Not sure about this one either. But you sort of need money to get stuff don't you? Not really important stuff (like love – see opposite), well apart from like food and shelter. But things like stuff. What sort of money you have and need depends on the planet you're on. If it's Menedlusia Mogginaxe then they use snow as money. Snow – imagine. So everything gets far more expensive in the summer. Especially ice cream.

Police Box

Big tall blue box thing that says 'Police Box' on it in big letters but which does not – generally – have a space-time machine hidden inside. Police boxes are surprisingly small.

Shopping

What you do with money (see earlier).

Shower

Like an artificial waterfall. You stand between these windows, or maybe in a bath, and let warm water rain on you and get you clean. Soap and things help, of course. Craig had a great one – I could stand under it for hours. Only problem is that you get wet.

Sleep

Not too sure about this one either. I think it's a human thing. Humans and tortoises. And maybe some other life forms. You close your eyes and partly switch off your brain – though some humans never really wake theirs up in the first place, if you ask me.

Tea

Tea is the best drink in the history of the known universe. You get these camellia sinensis leaves and grind them up very small, then add boiling water together with a dash of milk and maybe some sugar to create an infusion. Actually, it doesn't sound so good described like that. Tea is – well, it's just tea.

Television

Ah now, television is a way of wasting time by staring at a screen that converts received signals into pixels. The pixels make up a picture. Then the picture changes. It changes about twenty-five times a second, which gives the illusion that things on the screen are all moving about. It's a fantastic invention, except there's never anything good on. Except on Saturdays at about teatime. But the whole idea scares me, so I only ever watch from behind the sofa.

Myths and Legends

There are always stories. I love stories – we need stories. But it's often useful to know what's just a story and what's true. That gets tricky when something is sort of both. So here's some clues about things you might think are myths or legends but which may have a grain of truth in them. Perhaps.

Abominable Snowmen, the

Also known as the Yeti, these creatures are supposed to be like a cross between a man and a bear and live on the slopes of the Himalayas in Tibet. Mind you, the ones I met were giant furry robots created by an extra-dimensional alien intelligence. That was in Tibet. And on the London Underground.

Loch Ness Monster, the

Supposed to be a dinosaur left over from millions of years ago and living in the waters of Loch Ness. I mean, how likely is that? It's actually an alien armoured cyborg Skarasen brought to Earth by the Zygons who live off its milk and use it as a weapon. Obviously.

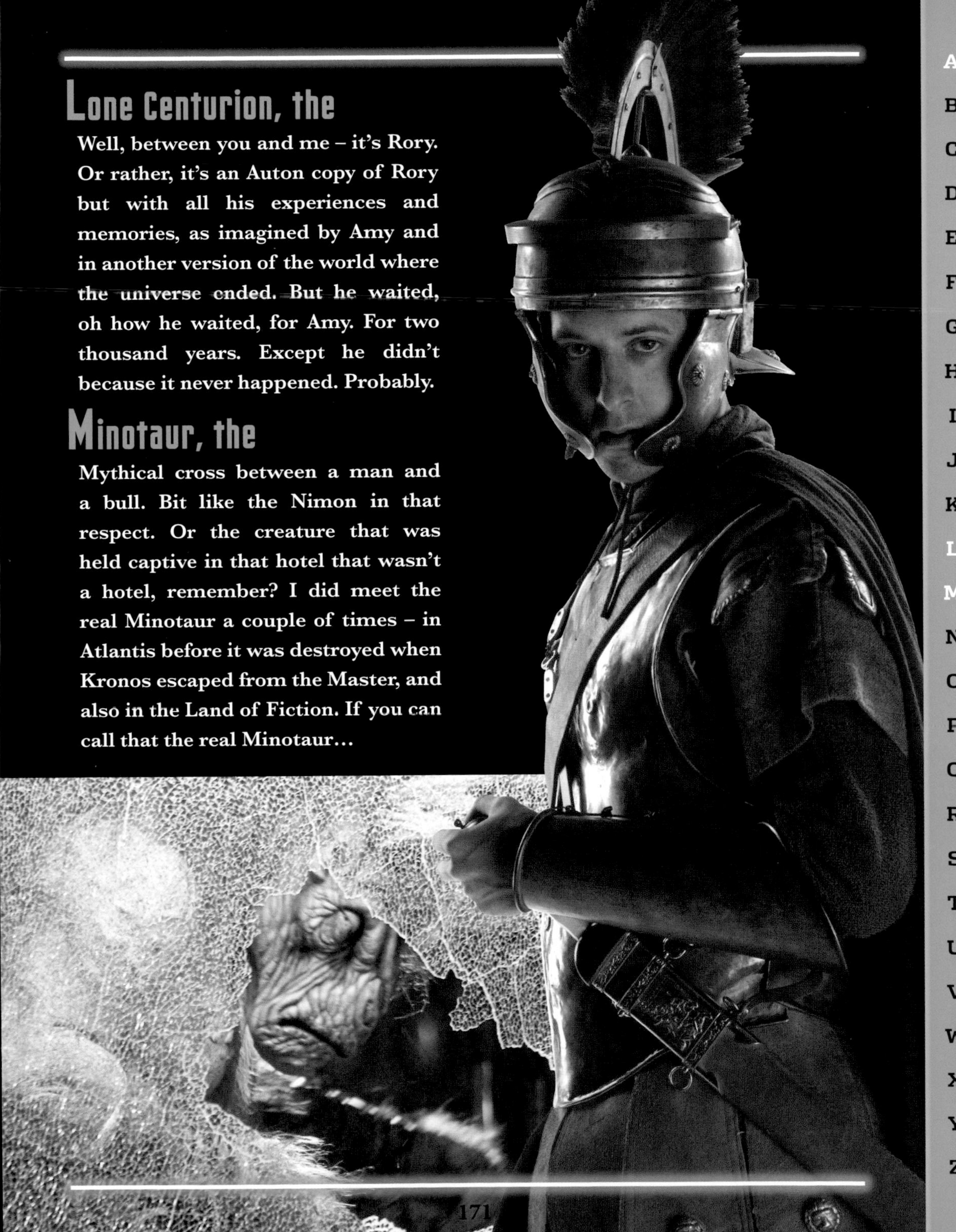

Lone Centurion, the

Well, between you and me – it's Rory. Or rather, it's an Auton copy of Rory but with all his experiences and memories, as imagined by Amy and in another version of the world where the universe ended. But he waited, oh how he waited, for Amy. For two thousand years. Except he didn't because it never happened. Probably.

Minotaur, the

Mythical cross between a man and a bull. Bit like the Nimon in that respect. Or the creature that was held captive in that hotel that wasn't a hotel, remember? I did meet the real Minotaur a couple of times – in Atlantis before it was destroyed when Kronos escaped from the Master, and also in the Land of Fiction. If you can call that the real Minotaur...

Pandorica, the

This is another legend I never really believed. Not until I got caught up in it – literally in this case. The Pandorica was like a giant box that was supposed to contain the most feared thing in the universe. Well that was just rubbish because what it was built to contain was me.

Silence Will Fall

Well who knows what that means? It's all to do with the question being asked, isn't it? That's what Dorium says anyway. The question that must never be answered. No doubt all will become clear – I'll let you know.

Snow White and the Seven Keys to Doomsday

Ah, now this one is just a story. Probably. A classic. I used to love that story. Stories like that made me want to go out into the universe and find out everything there was to know and see everything there was to see.

Snow White and the Seven Keys to Doomsday

The End

Three Little Sontarans, the

That one too. Though I never really warmed to the Sontarans, I have to say. And they're all little so that's a bit redundant – 'The Three Sontarans' would do just as well. I think they lived in the bottom of a treacle well, but maybe that was someone else...

The Doctor

What – a myth? A legend? What are you talking about? OK, so the Daleks call me the Oncoming Storm, but that's their problem. Am I a legend? Am I a myth? Or am I every bit as real as you and, er, me? Well, I guess that's one for you to decide. Though if you think I'm just a story someone made up, then you're in for a shock. And sooner than you think!

POLICE PUBLIC CALL BOX